THE SECULARIST HERESY

The Secularist Heresy

The Erosion of the Gospel in the Twentieth Century

Harry Blamires

SPCK
London

First published in Great Britain 1956 as *The Faith and
Modern Error* by SPCK
  Holy Trinity Church
  Marylebone Road
  London NW1 4DU
This edition published 1981

Copyright © 1956 © 1981 by Harry Blamires

Cover design by John B. Leidy

Printed in the United States of America

ISBN 0 281 03804 X

To
Robert Tindall

Contents

INTRODUCTION
to the American Edition of 1980

*T*he *Secularist Heresy* is a re-issue of my book *The Faith and Modern Error*, first published in the United Kingdom in 1956. Such a publishing event is unusual enough to call for comment, especially since *The Faith and Modern Error* was actually written in 1952, and the writer therefore looks back on it over a period of twenty-eight years.

There is much to suggest that we may now have reached a turning-point in Christian thinking. The launching of Servant Publications is itself one sign of change, and the re-publication of this book is, in its little way, another. For in respect of the subject of this book — the relationship between the Church and the world, between the Christian mind and secular society — the last sixty years have represented a phase which has now perhaps reached a watershed. We are increasingly hearing authoritative and penetrating criticism of the secularization and politicization of Christian values effected during this phase. "Relevance," one of the most overworked words in Christian controversy throughout the period, is ceasing to be a vogue word.

Complex historical, as well as theological, factors are involved in the changing emphases of Christian teaching and witness from generation to generation. I recall a time in my youth, in the 1920s and 1930s, when the challenge of "relevance" was acutely disturbing to the Christian worshipper. He

1

came away from church, perhaps having heard an excellent sermon on the evidence for the Resurrection or the doctrine of the Ascension, and then, looking around him, he wondered what connection it had with the world where queues of down-at-heels unemployed workers littered city centres and where victims of the Battle of the Somme, with half their faces missing, sold matches or bootlaces from their station in the gutter. What was called the "social gospel" movement was born out of impatience with pietism that seemed complacent about the glaring social injustices of the day.

The wheel has come full circle. I do not mean by this that there are no longer, in the early 1980s, comparable social injustices crying out to Christian conscience for remedy. I mean that the Christian worshipper is nowadays unlikely to come away from church wondering: Has that sermon got any connection with the secular world outside the church? He is more likely to come away asking: Has that sermon got any connection with anything other than the secular world? Has it led my thoughts where picking up a newspaper or turning on the television could not have led them? Perhaps the preacher's subject was "The Third World," or perhaps it was "Caring for Others." His address may have been noble, moving, and compassionate; and yet it scarcely said anything that a virtuous humanist could not wholeheartedly concur in. This does not mean that the sermon was not in itself worth preaching; but it points to a present danger in Western Christendom. Christianity is relevant to all aspects of life. Can we be so obsessed with being relevant that we forget to be Christian?

Current developments are pushing this question into prominence. And, as a result, a thesis which I propounded back in the 1950s suddenly assumes a startling immediacy. For at that time I persisted in pressing a question which everyone else seemed to be ignoring: How do you keep Christianity free of infection by the secularizing spirit of the age? Most thinkers of the time addressed themselves to the opposite question: How can you accommodate Christianity to the secular needs and trends of the day? If a writer asks the opposite question to that over which most of his contemporaries are agonizing, he can scarcely avoid producing a book with a rarity value all its own.

What was a valid question for a few apprehensive thinkers in the 1950s has now become, by reason of the developments I have mentioned, an issue that speaks to worried Christians all over the Western world. *The Faith and Modern Error* forecast this change. It made prophetic statements about what were likely to become the most urgent issues for Christians of the succeeding decades, and events have confirmed these prognostications. For instance, a passage on page 65 reads:

> Surveyal of contemporary movements in religious thought leads one to the conclusion that, in the near future, the dominating controversy within Christendom will be between those who give full weight to the supernatural reality at the heart of all Christian dogma, practice, and thought, and those who try to convert Christianity into a naturalistic religion by whittling away the reality and comprehensiveness of the supernatural basis.

Similarly, on page 149, the book foresees "the approach of an issue which will unite Christians across many barriers."

> And the issue, as I see it, is whether Christians who have a supernatural religion are going to be swamped by "Christians" who have only a humanistic philosophy of life.

These excerpts are not quoted for the purpose of proudly advertising the author's prescience. At the time when these statements were made, I could never have anticipated the virulent form which the epidemic of secularization would assume in attacking Christianity, nor the spiritual, intellectual, and moral nervelessness that would paralyze many supposed leaders of Christian thought. I could never have guessed how quickly the disease would spread, nor how many of the Church's supposed "doctors" would succumb overnight, to become themselves carriers of the plague. It is not pleasant now to look back on the intervening years and trace how, in some quarters, sclerosis of spiritual and intellectual fibre allowed even the great Christian virtue of love to be psychologized into free permits for adultery and promiscuity, for perversion and embryonicide.

Nevertheless my thesis correctly forecast the character of the disease if not its virulence — or, if I may say so, its absurdity; for evil is always absurd. And what could be more absurd than the spectacle of spokesmen for "Christian liberation" waving the banner of radical anti-authoritarianism while prostrating themselves with sickening servility before the authority of the World? This is the paradox of so-called "liberation" — that it is the way of servitude; the converse paradox to that of Christian obedience, which is the way of freedom in Christ.

A book written in the 1950s naturally draws illustrations from its own decade, and changing attitudes or fashions may have rendered some of these obsolete by 1980. There are a few trivial cases of such obsolescence. For instance, the expression "the hydrogen bomb" is used where now one would speak of "nuclear warfare." But perhaps only twice does the voice of the 1950s sound worryingly dated in the ears of 1980. The first such instance is the reference in the first chapter (page 25) to the "peace-time orderliness of contemporary civilization." Now, viewed historically, our twentieth-century environment in the West may still be comparatively secure. I do not myself feel worried for the safety of my family when I lock the door at night or when we walk about our locality after dark; and I trust most of my readers are equally happily placed. But it would be idle to pretend that urban conditions over our countries as a whole (the US and the UK) render our populations generally as free of worries over personal safety as they were perhaps twenty-five years ago. Indeed, far from stressing the peace-time orderliness of contemporary civilization, the prophet of today must surely discern the development of internal protest, dissension, and terrorism as the mark of a new historical phase. If the first six decades of our century were decades of international war or threat of war, the last decades seem more likely to be decades of internal violence and subversion.

And the violences may well stem, in the West, not from the repressive arm of intolerant government, left or right, but from upsurges against pacific authority by aberrant claimants to inner light. If external aggression has been our problem in the past, internal unrest will more probably be the menace of the future. We detect the beginnings of a phase in which challenges to reason, morality, and tradition are made in the name of perverted idealisms; even pornography and pederasty are defended by high-sounding rhetoric about individual freedom. And the weapons of internal blackmail, whether secret or public, whether by damage to others or damage to self, are perhaps going to prove less manageable than our nuclear arsenals. It is appropriate to make these points here and now because the danger is real that, if the Christian Church is sapped of its doctrinal virility and institutional sturdiness, Christianity itself may be perverted by some into an instrument of social and civilizational decomposition that has nothing to do with its proper call to self-sacrificial encounter with the world of materialism and unbelief.

Another adjustment is called for in relation to what is said about the intellectual climate of opinion on pages 101 to 104, in particular the confidence expressed that "modernism" (in the sense of doctrinal liberalism) is "out of date." This was written at a time when the buoyant orthodoxy of C.S. Lewis had made "modernism" look to many of us not only intellectually thin, but also "obsolete." The temptation to turn the tables is the besetting sin of polemicists, and I could not resist the paradox of proclaiming modernism no longer modern. The judgment was ill-considered. For indeed the whole book is an attack on modernism (in its widest sense) and if modernism had already been outmoded, then the book would have been superfluous. What the book ought to have done at this point was to distinguish between a particular aspect of modernism — which tried to dilute Christian teaching about the miraculous to fit the objections of sceptical scientism, and which had temporarily ceased to exercise many minds in public debate — and the broader operations of modernism as a force everywhere intent to accommodate the claims of a religion grounded in the supernatural to the naturalistic criteria of current secularism.

Having said what is necessary in introducing a book written in the 1950s to readers of 1980, I must also consider what comments are called for in presenting to the American public a book written in England with the British public in mind. I think only two points need to be made. The first concerns the strictures on the English Public School system on pages 68 and 69. The American reader needs to be aware that the English Public Schools, in spite of their name, are private boarding schools, independent of the national educational system. They charge high fees for tuition and residence, they inevitably cater to the well-to-do, and by tradition they have produced a social and intellectual elite exercising great influence in the spheres of government and administration, the armed forces, and even the Church of England. They have therefore been identified with what has come to be known as "the establishment."

The second point I would make for American readers concerns the use of the word "Church." In general it should cause no misunderstanding. The word is given a supra-denominational connotation. But, writing as an Englishman, I sometimes had the Church of England especially in mind. I think that I generally made myself clear by writing "Church of England" when I meant that. But if the reader is brought up with a jerk at any point in reacting to my use of the word "Church," perhaps he will be indulgent enough to recall that I

INTRODUCTION

was seeing things from a British point of view.

When Servant Publications decided to re-issue in the US my book *The Christian Mind,* first published in 1963 (and continuously available in print in the UK since then), they did so on the grounds that it was a timely book for the late 1970s, and its reception has justified that judgment. I have myself found that, whenever I have been requested to speak in public on the issues raised in *The Christian Mind,* I have been able to grapple most forcibly with the problems of today by combining ideas presented in this book with the thesis of *The Christian Mind.* For me the two books are inseparably connected. I deeply appreciate the gesture of Servant Publications in re-issuing both.

The decision to SPCK to reissue *The Faith and Modern Error* at home under its new title revives happy memories of my association with SPCK's former Director, Noel Davey, whose warm advocacy of my work was for long an important stimulus to me as a writer. I am grateful to the Society and to Robin Brookes, the present Senior Editor, for their continuing cooperation.

H.B.
1980

PREFACE

ONE OF the questions which this book tries to answer may be framed thus: In what ways is the Christian Message contaminated by the intellectual temper of the civilization in which it is now preached? Many others have tackled the problem of how to present the Christian Message in an idiom intelligible to the twentieth-century mind. I have addressed myself to the opposite problem—that of keeping the Christian Message free of corruption by twentieth-century habits of thought which are fundamentally hostile to it. Of course, these two problems are not opposed to each other in such a way that they cancel each other out. The problem of restating the Faith in living terms is one of presentation and linguistic interpretation. The problem of keeping the Faith free of contamination by false contemporary currents of thought is one of doctrinal soundness and doctrinal emphasis.

The reader will sense soon enough that much of what is said here springs directly from personal contact with modernist heresies which seem to me to knock the bottom out of Christianity. But I have attempted to render my strictures against current dilution of the Faith constructive, by setting them in the context of an essay which considers both the twentieth-century need and the kind of impact Christian teaching ought to have upon it.

PREFACE

As there is a certain amount of controversial aggressiveness in some portions of the book, I ought perhaps to express the hope that firmness will not be attributed either to bad temper or to ill-will. Certainly I ought to express the hope that nothing is said here which a layman ought not to say.

1

THE CONTEMPORARY SITUATION

WRITERS who undertake the very vital work of presenting a relevant Christian apologetic to our age are rightly much concerned with intellectual obstacles to acceptance of the Faith. It is interesting to speculate how large is the public catered for by this kind of apologetic and how large is the public to which it is totally inapplicable. This question is not raised for the purpose of depreciating the value of contemporary Christian apologetic by pointing to the limited range of its appeal. It is no use writing books except for those who read books. We may claim that those who read books—and are therefore at least mildly interested in intellectual questions—find much that is right for them in current Christian literature. In fact, Christian apologists generally may be said to cater fully for people who are already asking certain questions about life's meaning, or who are on the brink of asking them. In other words, they cater fully for those who are already believers, half-believers, or discontented unbelievers. They cater abundantly for uninstructed believers, for people on the brink of Christian self-committal, and for those who are uneasy in their atheism, their agnosticism, or their ill-defined theism.

It is right that Christian apologetic—at least in book form—should concentrate upon the public most likely to be responsive to the Christian Message. But it is undoubtedly true that, as a result of this concentration of intellectual appeal, the major problem of our day is overlooked. For the problem peculiar to our time is, not that large numbers of people are asking questions about life's meaning and trembling uneasily on the brink of Christian self-committal, but that by far the largest section of our population is completely without interest in the religious issue at all. They have not reached the stage of asking the questions which the Christian apologist answers. They have never truly recognized in themselves that deep discontent which only the peace of God can take away. They have not arrived at that phase of uneasiness which is so often a fruitful time for the sowing of seeds.

Now it is undoubtedly the duty of Christian thinkers to work out the right answers to the questions of the uneasy; above all to work them out in the present-day intellectual context, complicated as it is by huge advances in scientific knowledge at the specialist level, and by an enormous increase in confused and second-hand thinking at the popular level. But somehow we have to find a way of catering for the indifferent as effectually as we cater for the doubters and the questioners. What is the secret of those who are completely without interest in the religious issue? Is there any way of picturing their state of mind? Can we, for instance, characterize generally the state of mind of those who are totally uninterested in religion so as to distinguish it clearly from the states of mind both of those who question and of those who believe? It may even be the case that, in our own age, the difference between the interested and the uninterested in the religious issue is more significant than the difference between believers and unbelievers—more significant, that is, as a pointer to the true mental and spiritual condition of our generation.

It is clear from the start, of course, that this distinction transcends all differences of intellectual capacity. Learned men believe and question; and learned men are uninterested. The same may be said of ignorant men. Yet, if the Christian Faith is true, the Christian may expect the state of mind peculiar to those uninterested in the religious issue, whether they are learned or ignorant, to be productive both of moral evil and of intellectual confusion.

What is common to believers, uneasy questioners, and indeed to many thoughtful and earnest unbelievers, is a certain attitude to the finite. Finitude either has been, or is, a problem to them. They may or may not feel themselves to have solved the problem of finitude, but they have all, in some manner and measure, faced it. They may have faced it with the minimum of intellectual activity, or they may have tussled with it in learned researches of the philosophical or scientific order: but they have all alike been aware of it. This awareness may have come upon them as an abstruse intellectual problem or as a crude piece of primitive reasoning— Who made everything? What happens when we die? On the other hand, it may have come as a barely articulate, largely emotional response to some shattering fact of personal pain or bereavement. It may have come in sorrow or in joy; in response to the death of a child or to the birth of a child; in response to the cruelty of Nature or to the beauty of Nature; to the human refusal of love or to the human granting of love.

What is common to those who lack any interest in religion is a failure to recognize the finitude of the finite, and especially failure to accept man's own finite status for what it is. This failure is the source alike of moral evil and of intellectual confusion. All forms of moral evil have their roots in a tacit denial of human finitude—of the contingent and wholly dependent nature of man's existence. Pride in all its forms is always an implicit rejection of finitude. Man behaves as though he were not a dependent creature with a limited and temporary existence in a limited and temporal universe. Covetousness and greed for power both express the same defiance of finitude. Covetousness implies that the pursuit of earthly possessions is of ultimate significance: it implies that to possess within the finite is a state of fulfilment. This is nonsensical. There is no stability or security in possession within the finite order, where at any moment accident or death may strip or destroy. The pursuit of power implies that temporal sway and masterdom are an ultimate satisfaction: finitude precludes such satisfactions within its own domain. The same can be said of the pursuit of pleasure in self-indulgence, of the pursuit of knowledge as the weapon of temporal mastery, and of devotion to art as the hollow glorification of the transient and the sensual. In these pursuits, and in a thousand others, man conceals from himself the fact that finitude sets a term to all activities at the temporal level.

As moral evil testifies to man's failure to accept the fact of finitude in the deep regions of the will, so intellectual error represents man's failure to accept the fact of finitude in the intellect. The intellectual heresies of our day speak loudly of this failure. Humanism, however far-reaching in its idealism, assumes in man a power to determine his own destiny, which is not within the capacity of finite creatures. Moreover, it assumes a final validity in the establishment of a just and prosperous social order, which violates the thoughtful man's realization of the fact of death. Materialism does violence to the same sensitivities. It glorifies the temporal—the act of possession, the comforts and consolations of physical existence—as ends in themselves. By switching on the spotlight of humanitarianism—social justice and fair shares for all—it illuminates with an artificial halo the activities of man the animal—eating, drinking, and breeding.

Intellectual failure to reckon with the fact of finitude culminates in the Positivistic philosophy which proscribes as invalid any attempt even to conceive of finitude as a fact. For to conceive of finitude as a fact is to recognize the temporal and contingent nature of our universe and our existence within it. But the temporal and the contingent are impossible concepts except in relation to the eternal and the necessary. To conceive finitude is, in short, to conceive infinity. But infinity, eternity, and divine necessity are alike illegitimate concepts for the positivist. He will allow of no knowledge which is not descriptive either of the phenomenal world or of psychological states. Here indeed is the inner stronghold of modern man's failure to reckon with finitude. Here indeed is fully explicit that denial of the problem of the finite which is implicit in all moral evil and in all intellectual error. We may close our eyes to the problem of the finite; we may claim that the finite presents no personal problem; or we may cheerfully admit that the fact of finitude is a disturbing one which we endeavour at all times to forget. But the last fortress of defence against the ever-aggressive onslaughts of the infinite into human experience and into the human consciousness, must surely be the nihilistic dictum that the fact of finitude is not a thinkable thought.

The claim made here is that failure to accept the finitude of the finite is the Highest Common Factor in the varied states of mind which breed indifference to the religious issue. The man of learning who is too interested in his specialized research to think about religion, the labourer who is too interested in darts and beer, the clerk who is too interested in football pools, the statesman who is too interested in party policy, the shop-girl who is too interested in films, the company director who is too interested in high finance—they all have this common element in their prevailing mental visions, that man's finitude is not present to them as a realizable fact. This does not mean that they have each and all failed to take a particular philosophical view of the human situation. It means rather that they have failed *in any kind of way* to absorb into their mental systems the sense of humanity's imposed limitations.

The challenge of finitude may come to people in many diverse modes. It comes intellectually to the philosopher, the scientist, the historian, and the poet. The habit of lifting the eyes above the horizons of the immediate contemporary environment, in the study of any profound subject or the practice of any creative art, is likely to awaken the sensitive mind to the challenge of finitude. The philosopher is called upon to grapple with questions about the nature of reality, the meaning of existence, and the significance of human values, which are inevitably accompanied by this challenge. The scientists, face to face with the unimaginable movements of cosmic machinery, or with the extraordinarily complex evolution of organic life, can hardly fail to hear from time to time reminders of man's temporary status in a temporal universe. The historian, surveying the rise and fall of civilizations and cultures, is inevitably invited to comment upon the significance of individual man's achievements and aspirations within the headlong career of the passing centuries. The artist, shaping a vision of static beauty from contemplation of the fluctuating scene of human passion and human attitudinizing, must surely sense the frailty of all that men prize most in the transient order.

> O Love! who bewailest
> The frailty of all things here,
> Why choose you the frailest
> For your cradle, your home and your bier ?[1]

But the challenge of finitude, in its most acute intellectual form, is not for all men, not even for most men. Perhaps the number of men properly endowed to sustain it is not so large

[1] Shelley, "When the lamp is shattered", 1822.

as the number to whom modern education presents the challenge. But that is a different question. That the challenge of finitude comes more widely through less intellectual personal experiences which all men share is indubitable. The insecurity of his possessions brings the challenge to the rich man; the insecurity of his poverty brings it to the poor man. The awareness of continual good fortune brings it to the consistently healthy man; the menace of disease brings it to the sick man. The precariousness of health, wealth, and life itself is brought home at some point to every human creature. All who continue to survive, live to see previous generations sicken and die, and their own generation thinned out by the accidents of mortality.

Whole-hearted acceptance of this ubiquitous challenge of finitude seems to be the prelude to religious faith. If this is so, it explains why, in the long run, the magnitude of a man's intellectual equipment is irrelevant to the real quality of his faith in God. For the fact of finitude may be absorbed into the mental system, and absorbed into the will, with or without elaborate ratiocination. It would seem, indeed, that in every department of human experience, the challenge of finitude comes in a mode appropriate to that department. As the scholar cannot escape the challenge in an intellectual form, so the businessman cannot escape it in the shape of the insecurity of worldly prosperity and the failure of possessions to satisfy the soul. The doctor meets the challenge in the spectacle of suffering and death; the soldier, fisherman, and miner meet it in the daily risks of their calling; the farmer meets it in his dependence upon Nature's ministrations; the mother meets it in the pain and danger of birth, and all parents meet it in the vicarious risks of their children's expanding freedom.

To speak thus of the ubiquitous challenge of finitude, operating everywhere in modes appropriate to diverse realms of human experience, is merely to put in philosophical terms what the theologian means when he says that God's Love pursues our souls in an active and eager yearning at every turn of our mortal life. This is the poet's Hound of Heaven, tracking down our wayward fleeing souls, in a chase which can end only in our wilful surrender or our final escape from salvation.

Our theme here, however, is the apparently wholesale refusal of so many of our contemporaries to absorb into their systems this fact of finitude. Once the challenge is really accepted by anyone, then a definite attitude must emerge towards the religious issue. It may be an attitude of surrender to the Faith. It may be an attitude of prolonged, uneasy questioning that burdens the questioner with neurotic brooding and joylessness. It may be an attitude of undisguised hostility to the Christian tradition—of disgust with a Church which is alleged to care little about human misery and social injustice; of cynical contempt for any idealistic attempt to make sense of life's agonies and frustrations; of whole-hearted rejection of the idea of looking elsewhere for satisfactions which earthly life consistently denies; or even of uttered hostility to the God who designed this vale of tears for his creatures. Acceptance of the challenge may breed any of these states of mind, in men who are capable of expressing their ideas rationally and in men in whose souls surrender or rejection depends upon a wholly inarticulate inner direction of the will. The attitude which cannot possibly emerge from acceptance of the challenge is that of complete indifference to the religious issue. And it is such indifference that confronts us on all sides to-day.

We can only conclude that the bulk of our contemporaries never absorb the fact of finitude into their systems at all. The challenge meets them, in the diverse modes which have been illustrated, but they turn away and harden their wills against it.

People of a religious nature, who have absorbed into their systems the fact of man's finite status and accepted the Christian Faith, endeavour, with varying degrees of persistence and singleness of purpose, to adjust their wills to the demands of a God who transcends the finite order. The Divine Mercy is such that even a minimum effort at thus re-directing the will creates a habit of mind by which reminders of the challenge accepted meet them at every point of their experience. The round of day-to-day activities, of work, sociability, and family life, brings with it continual indications that earthly life, however good in itself, is a limited imperfect thing, beyond which the soul must aspire to higher and more lasting satisfactions. The extent to which these reminders of man's finite status are an uneasy or a joyful thing will depend, I imagine, on the progress made in the spiritual life. For most of us these reminders disturb more than they tranquillize. For the saints they are, no doubt, a movement in life's most joyful rhythms.

However that may be, people to whose consciousness the fact of finitude is daily present do not find it easy to conceive of states of mind from which the fact is habitually absent. And this presumably is why Christian apologetic is invariably directed towards the questioners and those vocally hostile to the Faith. For the questioners and the vocal enemies of the Church share with believers this common mental state of sensitivity to the fact of finitude. The indifferent, the uninterested, and the apathetic belong to another category altogether. Since they are habitually unaware of man's finitude, they can hardly be expected to respond to persuasions and exhortations which presuppose a fundamental sensitivity to man's finite status as the common inheritance of all mankind.

Since we ought to learn how to approach the indifferent with the Christian Message, it is important to analyse, if we can, the means by which this indifference is sustained. If the challenge of man's finitude pervades human experience as widely as we have suggested, how is it resisted? Clearly it is resisted in the face of the most tremendous counter-influences. All human suffering, privation, and loss point, we have said, to the fact of finitude. Indeed, the experiences of life which mystify so many people—pain, injustice, failure, and disappointment—are seen by the Christian as Divine encouragements to humble acceptance of finitude. Of course few Christians may have sufficient faith, few may have surrendered their wills so fully, that they can thank God for the mercy by which suffering disturbs man's false security. But all should be intellectually aware that this is how they ought to feel about it.

The fact is that certain human experiences, of joy and of pain, of prosperity and of adversity, come to some people with reminders of human finitude invariably attached to them. To others they come without any such accompaniment. Man's nature is of this kind: that he can experience possession, love, friendship, or power in such a way as to embrace in them the fact of finitude, or in such a way as to deny in them the fact of finitude. As with the joys of possession, love, friendship, and power, so it is with the sorrows of pain, privation, and bereavement. Before one can embrace finitude, one must recognize it. In order to deny finitude, it is only needful to ignore it.

In the process of thus ignoring finitude, man concentrates attention so feverishly upon the immediate object of terrestrial experience as to exclude from consideration the limitation, transience, and contingency of all objects given to sense-perception. "Feverishly" is the right word; because a balanced and rational devotion to a piece of constructive human work, to an artistic creation or to a loved person, can never exclude from consideration the fact that the object of experience is subservient to the limitations of the finite. This is one of those numerous cases where the rationality of the religious attitude to experience shows up the one-sided irreligious attitude in all its flaming irrationality. Philosophically speaking, it is the supreme ironical paradox of our era that feverish concentration upon the phenomenal order, which shuts out the recognition of its finite and contingent status, should be popularly considered as more rational than an allegedly "emotional" approach to the phenomenal world, which takes its finite and contingent status into account.

In the prevailing mental climate, then, man's finitude is disregarded. What are the peculiar conditions of modern life which nourish this disregard in the face of the counter-challenge pervading all human experience?

First among these conditions is undoubtedly the remoteness of modern urban communities from Nature. Man depends upon the ministrations of Nature for physical survival. However much the mechanisms of modern economic organization may attempt to conceal the fact from us, it remains true that physical survival depends upon the daily wresting of food, clothes, shelter, and warmth from the resources of the natural order. It is not easy for modern man mentally to connect the sealed cardboard packet of breakfast cereals with sowing and reaping, ploughing and harvesting, with the cyclic rhythm of the seasons and the proportionate blessings of sun and shower. It is not easy to connect the tinned beef with the growth and breeding of cattle—processes which are given, just given, to man, and which he cannot fully understand, let alone control. Indeed, our blindness and insensitivity about these absolutely free blessings of Nature lead to an extraordinary state of mind, comic and tragic in its perversity. For we imagine that we are dependent for daily survival upon the regularity of workers in the tinning factories. This is the sense of dependence that comes, if any comes at all.

As it is with supplies of food, so it is with the provision of warmth and clothing. When we turn on the gas fire, we may reflect about our dependence upon the workers at the gas works, and propaganda sees to it that we do not forget our dependence upon the labours of the miner. And indeed this increasing sense of man's dependence upon man is one of the real blessings brought by modern socialization of economic life. But do we reflect upon the sheer *giveness* of the coal? Again, we are continually reminded of the link between the clothes and materials which we purchase in the shops and the state of the textile industry in Yorkshire and Lancashire. We have really been taught our dependence upon looms, mill-girls, and cotton markets. But what of that more ultimate dependence upon the sheep's growth of wool and the fertility of the cotton plantations?

There is no doubt that the increasing sense of man's dependence upon his fellows, through the complex organization of production and distribution, has helped to numb the far more necessary realization of man's absolute dependence upon the given ministrations of Nature for the satisfaction of his basic physical needs. Where this sense of dependence upon Nature is acute, the realization of man's finite status inevitably accompanies it. It follows that, wherever the sense of dependence upon Nature is acute, there we find responsiveness to the religious issue. It may be a hostile responsiveness; but that is something very different from apathy. No case can illustrate this point more vividly than that of Thomas Hardy. Acutely conscious as he was of man's absolute dependence upon the seasonal ministrations of Nature, he was compelled to shape his sense of human bondage into a religious attitude. Churchmen fought his attitude; they are still fighting his attitude. But is there not, after all, something more pernicious to fight—that numbed unawareness of human dependence which precludes the very desire to come to terms with the universe?

A second condition of modern life which nourishes man's disregard of his own finitude is the prevailing practice of dealing with disease, birth, and death. The establishment of the modern system of hospitals and nursing homes, mental asylums and institutions for the crippled, the blind, and the dumb, has removed from the popular gaze a spectacle of mortality which perhaps man ought to contemplate far more than he does. Our friends and acquaintances are whisked suddenly away from our environment. There is talk of operations, mysterious hints of unknown possibilities—how rarely do we hear the words, "He is dying"!—and then the news of recovery, or death. Out of sight, out of mind. Hospital ceremony and etiquette are such that we even feel it our duty to keep away so long as the case is at all dangerous. We are encouraged to visit only those on the mend. The spectacle of recovery is what we are most often invited to witness.

In the same way a man may beget a large family and yet know nothing of birth. At the first sign of the labour pangs the taxi is called. The husband consigns his wife to the hands of a matron. Unless there are complications, and unless the labour proves to be a particularly long one, the next thing he hears is likely to be the news over the telephone that a healthy child has been born. Of course, the imaginative man is not likely to be unmindful of the pain and the dangers. But this awareness is neither so immediate nor so perturbing as the actual spectacle of birth. Above all it is less illuminating, less of a revelation. And surely birth ought always to be a revelation.

The removal of the spectacle of birth, disease, and death from the daily environment of the home undoubtedly encourages a state of mind marked by serious misconceptions.

One misconception is that birth, disease, and death are, in terms of general human experience, rare abnormalities. Of course we do not *say* that birth and death are abnormalities. But in so far as they play no part in the daily environment, they assume the qualities of curiosities in experience. They come within our ken as rarities which offend against the comfortable canons governing the easy tenor of our way. They offend against a tacitly accepted norm; a norm which is "real life". In the same way the establishment of institutions for the blind, the dumb, the crippled, and the mentally diseased removes beyond our daily horizon a spectacle which perhaps ought to serve as a regular reminder of man's dependence upon God for the *giveness* of his faculties, his limbs, and his health. There is no intention here to suggest that institutions of this kind are not thoroughly good. That they are great blessings to the afflicted is undeniable, and of course they are justified on all counts. Nevertheless we have the right to consider the effect upon the twentieth-century man of the fact that he is not confronted by the diseased, the maimed, the blind, and the insane in the ordinary course of life. He has to search out this spectacle of mortality, this potent reminder of man's dependent status.

It is probably true that the state of mind which we are investigating is further encouraged by the very real achievements of medical science in curing previously incurable complaints. The highly scientific treatment of all kinds of diseases, whether it is successful or not, is such a prevalent fact of our environment that a distinct attitude to disease emerges. This attitude is marked by the tacit conviction that disease has lost its mystery; that it is understood; in fact, that doctors are at last equal to it. With this growing conviction of man's mastery of disease comes inevitably a further dulling of the popular awareness of what man's transient finite existence is really like.

A third condition of modern life which nourishes man's disregard of his own finite status is the peace-time orderliness of contemporary civilization. So far as deeds of criminal violence are concerned, our civilization has reached a high point in the maintenance of civil law and order—a point not previously attained in history. The efficiency of our police forces is partly responsible for this. So too is our comparatively high sense of responsibility in the matter of personal violence. Indeed, if our civilization can claim credit for being *humane* to a degree unknown to previous civilizations, it is chiefly owing to its peculiar success in increasing human sensitivity to the evils of violence and brutality. The philosopher will, of course, question whether this sensitivity has been matched by sensitivity in matters less near to the heart of a generation obsessed by the quality of life at the level of the physical and the material. But that is a different question. We are sensitive about violence: we have organized our social life so as to reduce its dangers to a minimum in peace time. We can sleep in our beds in safety—even in remote parts of the country. We can make journeys in safety. There is the less pressure upon us to recall the transience of our earthly career. There is the less pressure upon us to commend ourselves to God before taking ourselves to bed or taking ourselves to the road.

At this point it may well be asked: Does not the menace of the hydrogen bomb cancel out the effect of all those features of contemporary civilization which nourish our sense of "normal" peace-time security? At first sight one might expect it to do so: but the human mind is such that a single encounter with a maimed fellow-creature, or with a limited but immediate danger, is more disturbing to personal security than a column in the newspaper promising possible destruction on a universal scale. Ask yourself—especially if you are a parent—whether the news that a homicidal criminal is at large in your immediate neighbourhood does not disturb you more than the latest assessment in the press of the damage that a dozen hydrogen bombs could do. The very magnitude of the new weapon's destructiveness somehow numbs our personal sensitivity. A single, lawless, lurking danger in the roads we and our children tread daily; that indeed is a thought which wrings from us a special silent prayer. But the possibility of a blinding flash, and the sudden extinction of all that lives over an area of twenty or thirty square miles; that is too wholesale and final to induce speculation about our personal prospects.

In other words, it is doubtful whether the menace of the hydrogen bomb does much to encourage that sense of personal precariousness which leads to recognition of man's dependent status. The words used in discussion of the new threat—"extinction" and "annihilation"—do not hint at a crisis which may strip the soul bare of earthly consolations. Rather they point to a total obliteration, untormenting in its suddenness and impersonal in its scope. The threat of the hydrogen bomb, as it is received generally by our contemporaries, does not raise a lot of uncomfortable personal questions. At one stroke it answers all that could be asked.

Lastly, as a contributory condition behind modern man's disregard of finitude, we must certainly reckon with the huge increase in the number of activities to which civilized man can give his attention. It may be argued that the peasant, say, of a hundred and fifty years ago, with little more to think about in his leisure time than the progress of plants growing in his own garden and of children growing in his own home, could hardly escape intermittent reflections upon the limitations of life within the natural order. But the inhabitants of twentieth-century cities and the inheritors of twentieth-century compulsory education are very differently placed. The attention and interest of modern man are absorbed by a thousand and one contrivances mass-produced by modern technology. Popular journalism, the cinema, radio, television, and the motor-car are perhaps the most obvious objects of popular attention. And we are not concerned merely with the way in which radio and automobiles exhaust the attention of those who listen, drive, and ride; we are also concerned with the way in which radio and automobiles exhaust the more intelligent and alert attention of those who tinker and construct.

It is impossible to particularize exhaustively in illustration of this immense fact. Activities of a sporting and athletic kind, professional and non-professional, absorb the attention of people to an enormous extent. Football, cricket, boxing, golf, horse-racing, dog-racing, motor-racing—these are some of the activities which, as spectacles or as active pastimes, absorb the interest of modern man. Attached to them are ancillaries such as bookmaking and football pools which number their customers in millions. However far we stretch our list, we must be careful not to suggest that these things are necessarily unworthy of human attention. For the purposes of our investigation, "highbrow" enthusiasms for opera, ballet, art, political controversy, butterflies, place-names, and folk-dancing are to be reckoned alongside less intellectual or less sophisticated enthusiasms. The simple fact is that more objects and activities, of varying degrees of worth, are offered to human attention and interest than at any previous point in history.

It is relevant to mention here that modern education intentionally sets out to cultivate such interests in the young. Rightly or wrongly, education is not nowadays considered to be fulfilling its proper function unless it equips its pupils with life-long interests in hobbies and arts which will make their future leisure tolerable to them. That this is a good thing may be deduced from the fact that man is most healthily occupied when his interest is given to things outside himself. But that this educational principle is an inadequate corner-stone for an educational philosophy will emerge from the argument of this thesis as a whole.

Having investigated some of the conditions of modern life which tend to nourish man's disregard of his own finite status, we may turn to the question: How is the habitual inner awareness of finitude to be stimulated in those insensitive to it? We have said that in every department of human experience the challenge of finitude comes in an appropriate mode. This is true even of the experiences listed above. Though the man who is not made deeply aware of finitude by the spectacle of suffering is unlikely to be made aware of it by a win in the football pools, yet nevertheless the challenge is present in both experiences. If anything ought to nourish awareness of the fluctuations of earthly fortunes, surely weekly subscriptions to football pools ought. Again, to take another example, the increasing elaboration of the complex mechanism linking the cornfield with our morning dish of cereals ought surely to deepen our sense of the precariousness of physical survival. Yet it seems to work in the other direction.

There are some of us for whom the spectacle of modern industrial civilization is more pregnant with reminders of life's precariousness than is the spectacle of village communities living close to the soil. Can we seriously reflect on our utter dependence, for water and warmth, upon the complicated underground systems of pipes and wires, without keenly sensing the precariousness of our essential supplies? Does not every increase in the elaboration of the system add to the possibilities of something going wrong? Again, the specialization of work in our economic structure is a frightening thing. Can thoughtful people easily forget nowadays that the activities by which millions of men make their living in administrative, cultural, educational, bureaucratic, and financial work, and work in the many public services, are all utterly dependent upon the labour in a few really productive activities: farming, mining, and manufacturing? Is not the whole fabric daily made more precarious by the addition of more and more ancillary activities? What do we now need to keep the miner hewing coal in the mine and the farmer ploughing his field? Labour for transport, for the manufacture of vehicles, for the maintenance of vehicles, for obtaining oil, transporting oil, distributing oil, and selling oil; labour for laying water, electricity, and gas to the home, for maintaining the services, for supplying the power; labour for manufacturing the radio set, for installing transmitters, for broadcasting, for publishing what is to be broadcast, for talking about what has been broadcast; labour for ensuring that labour is in supply, is properly distributed, is adequately paid, is kept in good health, is politically informed, is provided with the latest news, is given its chance in education, is entertained at the weekends, and so on.

I am trying to show that the spectacle of modern civilization ought to produce in the mind of man the opposite effect to that which it does, in fact, produce. The elaborate interdependence of all elements in its specialized organization ought to increase our sense of the precariousness of finite structures. Instead, it blinds us to the ultimate dependence of man upon the giveness of natural resources. We cannot see the wood for the trees. Yet an artificial plantation, elaborately laid out by man, testifies no less than does the wild forest or jungle to the given mysteries of germination and growth.

What are the marks of response to experience which reckons with finitude deep down in the heart? We may distinguish some of them quite simply. One is gratitude. This will mark in particular any experience of receiving gifts from the Divine Bounty manifested in the natural order. Another is admiration, or worship. This will mark in particular any realization of beauty or wonder in the earth and the creatures of earth. A third is humility. It ought to mark especially any keen experience of human dependence provoked by the taste of suffering or the spectacle of suffering and death. It ought also to mark every stage of advancing intellectual insight of the philosophical, scientific, or historical order. Anterior to all responses of gratitude, worship, and humility is the sense of human dependence, which is the ground of all three. And the full sense of human dependence is rooted in a keen awareness of man's finite status.

If, therefore, any kind of fruitful play is to be allowed to what are called man's religious impulses, the awareness of finitude must be stimulated. Now the process of stimulating this awareness is undoubtedly a process of disseminating discomfort and unease. It seems to follow that the Christian approach to the uninterested ought to concentrate much more than it does at present on pointing to the disturbing fact of life's transience and fortune's mutability. We would suggest that wayside exhortations not to worry, on the specious grounds that "it" may never happen, are not meeting the needs of twentieth-century man. Nor are sentimental reminders that a song in the heart eases life's daily burden likely to induce that hunger for spiritual nourishment which most of us desperately lack. Again, although there are occasions when the blackness of a cloud is all the blacker by reason of the sun's radiance which it obscures, we may question whether reference to the bright lining on its further side really exhausts the significance of the cloud. Lastly, although a single kind word to a human being in trouble is always worth uttering, it may be doubted whether its utterance ought to leave the speaker with the conviction that he has fulfilled his Christian obligations for the next twenty-four hours.

Of course, serious Christian apologetic does not deal in sentimentalities such as these: but it may be illuminating to ask just why these exhortations are irrelevant. They are irrelevant because they are, in their various forms, pats on the back. That they appear before us in the guise of specifically Christian exhortations is a pity, for, well-intentioned as they may be, they will do nothing to disturb us to that sense of dependence which is the prelude to faith. Publicly to administer pats on the back to our apathetic contemporaries can do little good. Indeed this kind of publicity may do harm, in that it can suggest that the real Christian Message is in fact on a par with the didactic sentimentalities of birthday cards, calendars, and quiet corners in the popular press.

The real trouble with such exhortations is that they are not in the least disturbing. Is Christian apologetic generally sufficiently disturbing? How often is it content merely with the attempt to equip the Welfare State with a conscience, and to ornament its organization of social justice with the embroidery of Christian charity? How often is it content to survey the social and philosophical developments of the last century, to show that twentieth-century civilization has exhausted the content of our predecessors' belief in progress, and to argue that we need some deeper philosophy to sustain our national prosperity in these less easy times? How often is it content merely to prove that the Bible is not after all out of date; that science opened its attack upon religion a little too soon; that now, after the labours of the critics have for the first time in history made the Bible really acceptable to intelligent men, God's Revelation is at last revealed in all its scientific ingenuity?

The last question of this series may be put quite briefly: How often is Christian apologetic content merely to answer questions? This is the crux of the matter. Because, if our diagnosis of the contemporary situation is sound, the way to touch the indifferent is not to answer questions, but to ask them. Are you satisfied with life? Are you satisfied with yourself? Can you face pain, bereavement, death? Is not your heart overcharged with desires which never seem to reach satisfaction, with hopes which life's experience so often seems to frustrate, with aspirations which life's horizons are too limited to contain? When you fell in love, when you married, when you first saw your first child, did you not then sense some fruition out of time, which you would move the earth to taste again? What if this life is but a testing, and that kind of joy made permanent is the reward of winning the test? What if the very act of perseverance in such a test endows you with the certainty that indeed such joy is given; given as freely as the gifts of Nature and the talents of the fortunate? What if the dissatisfaction, the despairs, the frustrations of your life were the very things that the Divine Love entered the world to shatter and destroy?

The real Christian Message must disturb. Sometimes it will disturb frighteningly, bringing as it does the sense of human weakness, sinfulness, and utterly abandoned dependence upon the Divine Mercy. But it will also disturb with lightning flashes of joyful illumination, wonderful hints of life's highest delights made perfect and permanent, delirious possibilities of experience such as poets dream of—of enjoying at one and the same time the vigour, buoyancy, and eagerness of youth and the insight, stability, and reposefulness of age. To sorrow or to joy, it is right to disturb. There must be Heaven in the Christian Message, and there must be Hell.

We can introduce Hell only in terms of human sin, suffering, and frustration made permanent and insoluble. We can introduce Heaven only in terms of human yearning satisfied and human delight made lasting and secure. In either case, be it noted, we take our starting-point from experiences common to all humanity. Whether our approach be intellectual or practical, the starting-point is the same. The intellectual approach to the indifferent starts from the facts of suffering and evil, aspiration and love; the practical approach starts from suffering and evil, aspiration and love, not as observed facts of human experience, but as actualities realized here and now. The appeal, in short, must be made to man as man, to man in his experience and knowledge of manhood, not to man in his professional capacity.

It is necessary to stress this point nowadays. Recently I was present at a discussion which seemed to me to reveal faulty thinking of a characteristically modern brand on this matter. The question was raised, whether it was of overriding importance to find a priest knowledgeable about machinery and science to be in charge of a new church in a housing estate built around a scientific undertaking. The estate contained a large proportion of scientists and technologists. Of course, as everyone agreed, if other things were equal, a scientifically-informed priest was to be preferred. But what if other things were not equal? Just how important was it to find a scientifically-minded incumbent? Almost all who contributed to the discussion firmly believed that no other kind of priest could possibly make an impression in such an incumbency. It was assumed that the priest ought to be able, above all else, to get into touch with the technologists and scientists on their own professional ground, to show in conversation that he shared their interests and enthusiasms.

In all humility I suggest that this view is utterly unsound. The only religious appeal which will touch the indifferent is a disturbing appeal, which starts from the fact or actuality of man's joys and sorrows. Only the appeal to man as man will raise the challenge of finitude. The buttressing of a man's reliance for satisfaction upon mechanical, technological, or scientific pursuits is not likely to bring this challenge near. Indeed there is grave danger that such buttressing will help to keep the challenge in the background. For we have seen that absorption in interests of this kind, healthy as it may be in itself, is one of the prevalent facts of contemporary life which lull man into complete satisfaction within the locked and limited bounds of finitude.

At the heart of the problem of twentieth-century man's indifference to religion lies the fact that the challenge of finitude is suppressed. Intellectually man seeks a coherent meaning within the closed finite order, and builds humanistic, mechanistic, and positivistic philosophies which treat the finite order as absolute and ignore its contingent and transitory status. Morally, man seeks final securities and satisfactions at the terrestrial level, and pursues earthly power, possession, and pleasure, as though they could never be withered by the hand of time or swept away by the hand of death. In short, man treats the finite as though it were infinite. He adjusts his mind and his will, not to the finite as it in fact is, but to the finite as he would wish it to be. Why is man guilty of this blindness? The Christian has a direct answer to this question. Man is a creature called to eternity: he is destined for infinity. It is right that his mind and his will should be adjusted to the infinite. What is wrong is that the finite should be disguised in a habit of permanence and security, thus to become the object of aspirations and strivings which it can never satisfy nor set at rest.

All man's endeavours to find the wholly good within the finite order thus bear testimony to man's vocation to the infinite. It is a bitter irony that the human pretensions which fabricate the false materialistic and humanistic philosophies of our time should arise from that very impulse towards an infinite good that they ultimately seek to suppress or destroy. It is an irony even more bitter that man's pride, covetousness, and lust for pleasure and power, should be perversions of potentialities for fulfilment and glory which are man's peculiar blessing and inspiration. It is man's especial tragedy that the God-given impulse to transcend and transfigure the finite should be perverted into a demonic zeal for disguising the finite as absolute. Yet the bitter irony is paradoxically our surety and our hope as well. For without that inner demand for security and rest, which in its perverted expression lures us to the feverish pursuit of earthly treasure and pleasure, natural man would be unaware of his high calling. The paradox is indeed a powerful one. Intellectually speaking, the finitude of the finite, which is the coping-stone of scepticism, is also the corner-stone of belief. The finitude of the finite, which speaks to the atheist and agnostic of a mindless and meaningless cosmos, speaks in the same breath to the Christian of the reality of the Infinite. Ultimately the purely intellectual proofs of God's existence are one and the same with the proofs that he does not exist at all; the same, that is, in their reference to the surveyed experience of man. Upon the question, which is the rational interpretation of this experience, Christian and atheist disagree.

It is not surprising that St Thomas Aquinas's Five Ways of proving God's existence by natural reasoning amount in fact to an assessment of the relation of the Infinite to the Finite. The position of the modern Christian apologist, who argues within the domain of Natural Theology, is substantially the same. A. E. Taylor's massive and irresistible Gifford Lectures, *The Faith of a Moralist*, provide a characteristic modern treatment of the same issues. But then, what serious philosopher, or what serious poet has not been tormented with the problem of the finite? To the sceptics the arguments of the centuries must be a harrassing source of confusion and bewilderment. The Christian sees man's sorrows and joys, his evil and his good, his successes and his failures, as all alike evidence of man's lot as the inheritor of the infinite grappling with the finite; the Christian alone therefore can pluck out the heart of man's experience and wisdom. For to the Christian there is neither poet nor philosopher—believer or pagan, saint or debauchee—whose recorded aspirations and frustrations do not point to the same conclusion. There is many an argument in a library of philosophy which is designed to lead men to faithlessness and despair. But, accept the Christian vision, with its peculiar interpretation of the relationship between finite and infinite, and there is not a word therein which cannot be seen as testimony to Christian truth.

One last point remains. If the challenge of finitude is the key which opens the door to faith, then an intellectual climate which ignores this challenge can only help to sustain indifference. In short, if the challenge of finitude is to be made intellectually, our cultural and educational life must be alive with the questions which raise the religious issue. There is no such thing as a specifically Christian education, for instance, unless it introduces at every point the facts of the transience and contingency of finitude, and the absolute demand to transfigure and transcend the finite order. In every domain of intellectual life—humane, scientific, aesthetic, philosophical—the inadequacy of the finite and the reality of the infinite are not just relevant facts, but dominating facts. Unless they are accepted as dominating facts, the intellectual life cannot lay claim to be under an effective Christian inspiration. This is as true of higher research in the universities as it is of the first lessons of the nursery school. When Christian educationalists themselves accept this truth and see its implications realized in their practical work, there will be a change in the popular attitude to religion. It will be a change so enormous and momentous as to form one of the great revolutions of history. The challenge of finitude will be made at every level of educational work. And, as one result, a greater number of noisy sceptics, aggressive atheists, and argumentative agnostics will almost certainly be produced. There will also, one is bound to believe, be an increase in the multitude of zealous and thoughtful believers. Most significant and certain outcome of all: mass popular indifference to the religious issue will be a thing of the past.

2

EVASION OF THE GOSPEL

THE GOSPELS are shot through with the sheen of the supernatural. No one who is unable to take the supernatural seriously can make sense of the Bible. Yet our present age is supremely hostile to the supernatural. Our intellectual life is dominated by naturalistic philosophies which accord a quite unwarranted significance and universality to the techniques and conclusions of natural science. Our social life is perverted at all points by the attitudes and devices of a technology devoted to the mechanical exploitation of matter and mankind. Our moral life is coloured by the materialistic presuppositions of an ethos pledged to the propagation of physical well-being and prosperity. Naturalism, mechanism, and materialism permeate our thinking. If we are Christians, we find it appallingly difficult to maintain in awareness the reality of the supernatural. The presuppositions of the society in which we dwell offer defiance after defiance to the idea of the supernatural. The world is at war with the faith to which we are pledged.

We have represented the need to meet this situation by a rigorous Christian assault upon servitude to the finite. Naturalistic, mechanistic, and materialistic presuppositions can be undermined only if Christian evangelism continually points to the inadequacy of purely finite ends and satisfactions. This must be the Christian response to the fact that our faith, rooted in infinitude, faces a civilization which is locked within the temporal and the finite. Having acknowledged this incongruity of an infinite demand upon a society strangled by finitude, it is our business to ask whether the presentation of the Christian Message generally remains untainted and unadulterated by the presuppositions of the earthbound society in which we live. None of us can claim to be utterly exempt in his moral life from the taint of mundane evaluations which make a mockery of God's transcendent reality. Few of us can pretend to be generally free in our intellectual life from subservience to fashionable and ephemeral criteria which weaken the comprehensiveness and coherence of the Christian synthesis. In this situation, fallible and weak as human intentions are, do we generally succeed in keeping the Christian Message itself untainted by standards of judgement and evaluation which are rooted in naturalistic and materialistic presuppositions?

At first sight, this may appear to be a question of theoretical interest alone. On deeper inspection, it turns out to be the most crucial issue of all. "If the salt lose its savour, wherewith shall it be salted?" As long as humanity preserves, in the Christian Message, the true challenge of the eternal, there is always the possibility of shaking men free of subservience to finitude. If the message itself is corrupted by the ideas it is called upon to combat, then indeed we are in a parlous condition. The urgent necessity to proclaim the Christian Message in an unchristian world is obvious. But, in a logical sense, it is subordinate and secondary to the need to keep the Christian Message Christian.

A curious element in the temper of modernity helps to confuse this issue. It is the prevalent belief that the cherishing of ideas and ideals utterly exalted above prevailing contemporary practice is the mark of hypocrisy. On this point we have probably much to learn from the temper of medieval Christendom. Historians never weary of pointing to the incongruity between the faith professed by the medieval Church and the moral laxity of so many medieval Churchmen. A tacit accusation of hypocrisy hangs in the air. Without wishing to condone the kind of moral laxity referred to, or to minimize the evil of incongruity between practice and profession, we may rightly question whether our squeamishness is always well grounded in this particular. Does a promiscuous society mend matters by abandoning the ideal of monogamy? Of course we could praise the medieval Churchmen more fervently if they had maintained a higher level of morality. But men are men, and sin is always among us. Would we rather that they had achieved congruity between precept and practice by lowering their theoretical standards to accord with their sinful habits? Of course the medieval emphasis upon preserving the integrity of the Faith, intellectualized in dogmatic propositions, was out of tune with the prevailing weaknesses of many Churchmen. But surely this emphasis was in itself good. As long as the Christian Message remained uncorrupted, there was hope that it might strike home. Indeed, the emphasis upon the integrity of the Message itself showed a concern for posterity which we might profitably emulate. The Middle Ages handed on to us a body of doctrine scrutinized, analysed, and illuminated so profoundly that all succeeding ages have cause to be grateful for the legacy. Medieval Christians banqueted on some exotic, even perilous dishes; they tended to eat within locked doors; they were capable of slaying their fellows at the feast; but at least they preserved the flavour of the salt.

This point does not herald a recall to medievalism. Its sole purport is to illustrate the necessity of keeping theoretical foundations clear and pure. Our very dread of hypocrisy may become a snare to us. It will certainly become so if it leads us to underestimate the importance of vigilance against compromises of the faith made to suit the temper of the time. And the temper of our time is such that it will seduce Christians most insidiously in this direction—towards the minimizing of the supernatural reality in which the Christian Message is wholly rooted.

This total entanglement of the Christian Message in the supernatural is a disturbing fact. It is, quite literally, a shocking fact. And if the Christian Message does not shock, then the message itself is probably distorted. A generally comforting "Christian" Message, which neither shocks nor disturbs, is a Christian Message that has managed to disentangle itself from the supernatural. There are those among us who are experts in the art of thus disentangling the Christian Message from its own essential centre, those who present the supernatural, not as permeating the Christian challenge, but as providing a background to it. It is convenient to make the supernatural—the fact of a controlling, creative Deity in a life beyond time—a background to a few simple rules for moral conduct and a few pieces of good advice for the amelioration of social conditions. A background has this especial convenience, that it remains still a background however far back it is pushed. And we must admit that the reality of the supernatural is often a dim, vague, and remote background against which a supposedly Christian programme for personal and social behaviour is presented.

Let us therefore note how the fact of the supernatural interpenetrates the Christian Message, both as a personal challenge and as a description of our general human situation. The personal challenge of Christianity is the call to baptism and regeneration through grace. It is the call to repentance and self-surrender. Each of these five crucial words—*baptism*, *regeneration*, *grace*, *repentance*, and *self-surrender*—brings us face to face with the supernatural. A call to altruistic behaviour and humanitarian effort does not necessarily involve the supernatural at all. One may desire to live well, and strive to do so, without reference to the supernatural. But baptism is from above, regeneration is rebirth into a life dominated by the spirit, grace is the gift of the Holy Spirit. You cannot be born again except into a new life; you cannot repent except before some Person; you cannot surrender yourself except to some Will. The Christian moral challenge is summed up in the vocation to do the will of God. A life of obedience to the Will of God is a life guided and inspired from the supernatural.

Moreover, as a description of the human situation, the Christian Message is equally permeated by the fact of the supernatural. For the Faith teaches more than that Christ in history died and rose again. It teaches Redemption as a present fact, transcending the sequence of historical time. The conquest of sin has been achieved. A new Covenant has been established, the gulf between God and man bridged in the Incarnation and Sacrifice of Christ. Perhaps it is clear now why a strictly "scientific" approach to the miracles recorded in the New Testament is beside the point. Such an approach prejudges the whole issue. For it assumes that the intervention of the supernatural in the natural, if it took place, was an isolated phenomenon at a particular point in history, and nothing more. But Christianity teaches that what happened uniquely and supremely in the historical events of Christ's life is yet happening all the time. The fact that God gives himself in atonement for human sin is a fact which transcends the sequence of historical time. In the Church survives the fact of Incarnation, and she calls us daily to give ourselves in repentance that we may share the grace of atonement. The Church therefore witnesses to—even manifests—the impingement of the supernatural on the natural order as a present fact. The Prince of this world is judged.

It is therefore, to say the least, extremely presumptuous of us to imagine that our chief duty is to judge the Prince of this world—or even to strive, in our own right, to make ourselves good. Our primary duty is to accept the reality of the supernatural as manifested in Christ, to accept redemption and atonement through grace freely offered. In short, we cannot *begin* to be Christians except by deference to the supernatural. The reality of the supernatural is not something which we can put off, in the first stages of Christian growth, as an embarrassing feature which can be faced later on, and its validity investigated as Christian experience develops. There is no Christian experience without the supernatural. This is true of personal life, of social life, even of intellectual life. In the realms of morality, community, and intellect, the challenge of Christianity is the voice of another world.

Christianity comes, not to corroborate, but to transfigure the desires and purposes of natural man. And in that antithesis is comprehended all that this chapter has to say. Corroboration is one thing, and transfiguration is a very different thing. The heresy of our day, which we are here attempting to define and to combat, is the heresy of transforming Christianity into a corroborating religion. A corroborating religion ornaments the moral life with a supernatural sanction. Christianity does more than this: it transfigures the moral life with a supernatural penetration. A corroborating religion promises a life after death for a natural course dutifully played out. Christianity offers more than this: it offers here and now the entry upon a life of the spirit lived within the reality of the eternal. Again, a corroborating religion offers a motive for humanitarian labour, service to the community and the generations which will follow. Christianity offers this and more: it permeates every personal striving for the good of mankind, declaring it an obedience to the Divine Will and the manifestation of an impulse from the Holy Spirit. A corroborating religion asserts that our good deeds have the blessing of God. Christianity goes much further: it declares that man's good deeds are willed by God, inspired by God, and ultimately, indeed, effected by God. Finally, a corroborating religion gives the support of orthodox dogma to the discoveries of the intellect and the visions of the imagination: whereas Christianity reveals every truth and every uncorrupt dream of man as symbolic of some element in the nature of God. God is not just the remote end nor the remote first cause, not just the sanction, the explanation, nor the excuse. God in Christ is the Way, the Truth, and the Life. If there is life at all, truth at all, progress at all, there is the Spirit of God— not only calling, guiding, sanctioning—but indwelling at the very heart of the human impulse and aspiration.

It is not enough, then, to present the Christian Revelation as a corroboration of the theistic point of view, or of the ethic of altruism and service; as a blessing upon the idealism and zeal of humanitarianism, or upon the individualism of liberal democracy. The Christian Faith does not exist merely to bolster and buttress the less selfish aspirations of secular society. To regard it thus is to treat the supernatural order as a mere appendage to the world of nature. The message of the Kingdom is not a running commentary on the heroic struggle of ethical man: for the supernatural does not derive its meaning from the natural. It is the other way round. There is no good that is not derivative from the God whom the Christian serves: there is no good in which God ought not to be worshipped as sole cause, sole inspiration, and sole end.

In attacking the kind of thought which reduces Christianity to the dimensions of a corroborating religion, we are not of course assaulting a lie: we are uncovering a gross understatement. For the Christian Revelation does indeed corroborate all that is good in the moral, social, and intellectual life of mankind. But there is much more to be said than that: and the trouble is that all too often it is not said. Too often we are made to feel that the Christian's earthly career proceeds under the tranquil favour of a divine connivance, when we ought to be called to the enlivening and transfiguring of our daily course by the breath and fire of a divine incursion.

There is no attempt here to depreciate the natural. Indeed our quarrel with those who reduce Christianity to a religion of mere corroboration, is that they have too little care for the dignity of the natural. In failing to reckon with the prevenience of the supernatural, they damage the status of the natural, whose true vocation is to be, not just regulated, but redeemed, not just temporarily approved of, but eternally transfigured. You do not cast a slur upon man's activities within the natural order by declaring that they ought to be transfigured by a supernatural penetration, any more than you cast derision on a house by asserting that it ought to be lived in. Our concern is, not to belittle the natural life of man, but to magnify and exalt it, declaring it fit to be permeated through and through by the power of the Holy Spirit. Every insistence upon the pre-eminence of the supernatural is a claim of profounder significance in the natural. The natural life of man was not suddenly depressed in status when God himself condescended to live it: it was for all time exalted and transformed.

For God was not content to tell us, from a distance, how to jog along in finitude. He did not merely provide us with encouragement and promise us something better if we stay the course. God chose instead to live the life we have to live, eating and drinking and sleeping, walking and talking, the life of laughter and joy, suffering and desolation. The call to live in the power of the Resurrection is a call to renew in ourselves the reality of Incarnation every day of our lives.

We are not invited to accept an external code; we are asked to submit to the direction and inspiration of indwelling Love. God does not want to advise us from afar, but to possess us from within. He could have advised us from afar without the Incarnation and without the coming of the Comforter. He chose another way.

The centrality of the doctrine of the Incarnation in Christian dogma is thus the only sure safeguard against error. It is the manifest assertion of the Divine Initiative. And we call into question the Divine Initiative, if we exercise our presumption in casting God for the rôle of Celestial Watch-Dog, when he is in truth the active, insistent Hound of Heaven, pursuing us down the arches of our temporal years. This life of appetite and sensation, of thought and reflection, must be his. This life of social experiment, cultural progress, and humanitarian endeavour must be his: his because he dwells in the hearts and guides the wills of those who think and feel and fabricate. That is the religion of Incarnation. With every added emphasis on the Divinity of our Lord and on the supernatural vocation of mankind, it increases the stature of our earthly labours after justice, peace, and prosperity.

We shall lose our world if we attempt to save it by our own power. If we try, of our own resources, to preserve intact this little corner of finitude, pausing intermittently to nod our acknowledgement towards God's detached omnipotence, then we refuse the eternal inheritance to which we are called. It is betrayal to use the Christian Faith merely to decorate, where it ought to determine. It is blasphemy to ask God to bless, when we have denied him the chance to guide and direct. Our supernatural vocation is logically prior to our earthly affiliation. If we first stake our claims within nature, and then try to drag in God to justify and sustain them, we turn the religion of Incarnation upside down. To treat the Christian Revelation as an ornament, an additional buttress, or a justifying hypothesis is to deny the reality of the Incarnation.

We may consider one or two of the themes in the contemporary presentation of the Christian Message which seem to express this kind of error. One is the familiar and—so far as it goes—just claim that Christianity offers the remedy for twentieth-century *malaise* and disillusionment. How often have we heard, and read, learned and penetrating surveys of the development of western civilization in the past hundred and fifty years, surveys designed to present the Christian Faith as a last refuge for despairing man? We are told of the glories and shames of nineteenth-century civilization—of the rapid expansion of industrial activity, colonization, and the exploitation of the world's natural resources. The movement of material expansion and increasing economic prosperity at the national level was accompanied by an optimistic philosophy of progress which saw the whole of creation gloriously hastening forward to one far-off divine event. We are told how the discoveries of scientists in the technological field opened up ever more numerous roads to industrial enterprise and commercial enrichment. Yet there was a fly in the ointment. For science made other discoveries too before the century was out, and others yet again before the First World War came upon us. The theory of Evolution shook the foundations of Christian Revelation, so solidly established, at least in the Protestant world, upon the authority and veracity of the Scriptures. The theories of the psychologists cast doubt upon the Christian version of man's predicament, as a fallen creature rooted in sin and called to self-conquest.

And so, we are told, both the positive and the negative aspects of nineteenth-century thought came to climax and collapse in the first quarter of our own century. The movement towards material prosperity was checked by excessive international competition and by the drying-up of export markets. Colonial peoples rebelled against imperialistic exploitation abroad, and Labour organized itself against capitalistic exploitation at home. At the international level, competition culminated in two world wars. At the national level, proletarian rebellion produced the demand for Welfare States and fair shares for all, just at the moment when there were no longer enough shares to go round. The optimism of liberalism died in two world wars. The liberal philosophy of progress died with the drying-up of export markets and the shortage of raw materials. The individualism of liberalism petered out in the demand for organized and imposed security and welfare for all.

Yet, it is claimed and rightly, if the philosophy of progress and individualism died, the philosophies of mechanism and materialism were mortally stricken too. Biology was discovered not to have shaken anything fundamental in the Christian Revelation. Freudian psychology was shown not to have established any sure science of behaviour acceptable as a rational alternative to the Christian ethic. Meantime physicists discovered an element of indeterminism at the heart of apparently organized matter. In short, not only the alternatives to the Christian Faith have departed from us: the respectable objections have gone too. Moreover, in the spectacle of prevalent despair, cynicism, disillusionment, and moral disintegration, we can now inspect, as in the laboratory, the results of an experiment in popular revulsion against Christianity. The spectacle is not a pleasant one. Everything points to a return to God.

This kind of appeal is familiar to many of us. The almost overwhelming quantity of truth expressed in the argument and the exhortation must not blind us to that small but crucial element of error which it is our business to seek out. The exhortation implies that Christianity is peculiarly the religion for our day. So it is. It was also peculiarly the religion for the most prosperous decades of the nineteenth century. And it will be peculiarly the religion for the twenty-first century at its most glorious, even if the unification of the political world and the exploitation of atomic energy as a source of industrial power produce an era of prosperity and material well-being unmatched in history. The Christian Faith has to be accepted because it is true, not because all other known alternative philosophies have proved false or inadequate. The Christian Faith is not just the best working hypothesis for an age of crisis and despair. It is the truth which bestrides the centuries and their civilizations.

Yet I have listened more than once to the sermon roughly summarized above—and listened to it on the lips of men of such eminence that their words ought to be pondered. And, indeed, they raise some disturbing questions. Does it require a skilful historical survey of the trend of events in the world of politics, commerce, and intellect, during the past hundred and fifty years, in order to justify the contemporary claims of the gospel of Christ? Is it necessary to claim that we are the victims of such a coincidence of complex historical cross-currents, in order to excuse our recourse to the Faith of Christendom? Is Christianity a drug of such doubtful efficacy that we must be assured of our age's incurable sickness, before we take the risk of prescribing it? Is God to be advertised as a substitute for commercial prosperity, and the Christian life as a national antidote to post-war depression, slump, and spleen?

It is always disquieting to meet with this increasing tendency to recommend the Christian Faith merely as a means to an end, whether the end be social harmony or personal integration. For wherever this tendency exists there is a taint of materialism and a corresponding failure to appreciate the total entanglement of the Christian Message in the supernatural. The tendency is to be regretted, not because it implies the desirability of some purely temporal good, but because it treats Christianity as a subordinate *instrument* for achieving it. Whether the good be social or personal, we have the right, perhaps even the duty, to pursue it; but we have no right to recommend Christianity *simply as a device for attaining it*. We must not *exploit* our Faith by advertising it as a technique for achieving earthly satisfactions. The Faith is not a recipe and not a programme. It is a Way. Recipes and programmes are made to help you to carry out earthly jobs successfully. But a Way is something you walk in.

Thus, to preach the Christian Message as a recipe for world brotherhood and peace can be both erroneous and dangerous. Surrounded as we are by movements towards ecclesiastical unity between Christians of various nations and denominations, we must be wary lest the Christian Message is converted into a programme for developing international collaboration. The ecumenical movement is much talked of nowadays. No doubt the responsible leaders of this movement are fully aware of the true nature of the Christian Message. But the movement generates enthusiasm and activity over a wide area, and some at least of this support appears to be dominated by the overriding desire to manufacture a piece of universal machinery for safeguarding peace and brotherhood in the abstract.

Now the Church itself has been mercifully preserved from degenerating into a machine. The Church is an institution, whose unity is proclaimed by the operation of a single indwelling Spirit. The outward marks of this unity are not features of mechanical organization—such as committees—but common rites and common creeds through which the worship and faith of united persons is expressed. Moreover, these rites themselves take their validity from the operation of the Holy Spirit from above. The Church is a unified Body only through the operation of the Holy Spirit. It is, of course, the desire of every Christian that there should be, outwardly and inwardly, One Church. This unity—the unity of a single institution—can grow only by the increasing acceptance of common rites and creeds. We cannot do without the work of those who remind us of the need for this unity and who strive to make its realization more attainable. But the expenditure of zeal and energy (and money) in constructing interdenominational mechanisms which impose a façade of unity from without, is likely to divert effort and resources from the main task of evangelism—which is to present the personal call to repentance and regeneration. Joint committees and conferences, as such, are mere mechanisms. They cannot assume for themselves the quality of the institution, which is unified by the Spirit. Of course, they may hasten the growth of real inner unity; but this will only be possible if the members of such committees realize the purely mechanical function of the bodies on which they sit.

To treat the World Council of Churches as though it could command an allegiance transcending, and even to some extent nullifying, an allegiance already owing to a denominational body—this is to treat a mere piece of machinery as though it were a living institution with its own existential centre. When this kind of attitude is adopted, the dangers of the ecumenical movement become apparent. So too when interdenominationalism is transformed into a glorious new recipe for the spread of general good fellowship.

Once again it must be said that there is no intention here to depreciate natural good or secular idealism. *Because* we are Christians, we strive for international peace, better social conditions, inter-racial equality, harmony between workers and employers, and economic justice for all. But we must not recommend the Faith simply *on the grounds* that it will

51

produce these temporal benefits. We preach the Faith because it is true: because God so loved and loves the world.

There is also a tendency to-day to recommend the Christian Faith as a remedy for the tensions and frustrations of the disordered individual psychosis. Here again danger arises when the Faith is regarded as a means to a purely temporal end—namely, the attainment of a sense of personal well-being. We have heard a dose of religion prescribed for neurotic patients rather as an orange-juice diet or a month at the seaside is prescribed for others. Even the sacrament of penance and absolution has been recommended—not as a way to God's mercy through humble self-committal—but as a likely recipe for restoring the self to confident joy in living. Indeed the true Christian Message shades off imperceptibly into dangerous heresy in this domain.

Alarming implications can sometimes be detected in the words of those doctors of the spirit most prone to alliances with the psychiatrists. One hears the clear and illuminating vocabulary of Christian morality and Christian conversion thrown overboard in favour of the jargon of psychology. I have even heard warnings against the unhealthy morbidity of nourishing guilt-complexes uttered as meditative preludes to traditional prayers. It is doubtful whether the simple Christian call to repentance and renewal is illuminated for the present-day congregation by pious contemplation of the function of the subconscious. It is even more doubtful whether the moral tension of man's struggle between Heaven and Hell can be resolved in prayer most fruitfully after a devout meditation upon the influences of heredity and environment. Not this way self-surrender lies.

The presumed need to introduce this new vocabulary pre-supposes the inadequacy of the old one. Christian teachers most prone to this kind of thing unwittingly give the impression that psychology has something new to tell us about man's moral predicament and his spiritual needs. But whatever modern psychology has in fact to tell us—and many of us suspect that it is not very much—it certainly does not include the fuller revelation of man's situation in the light of the eternal. Yet perverse doctrines grow upon this untenable presupposition. One is the idea that psychology is gradually discovering the Christian Faith for us. The progress of the science has been slow as yet, it is grudgingly admitted, but already eminent psychologists are "moving near to Christianity". In a few more years, when the conditioned reflex has at last been fully explored and the doctrine of behaviour freed from deterministic overtones, then the grand *rapprochement* between religion and psychology will mark an end to the era of superstition. Not infrequently there is conjured before the mind's eye the picture of the Pope publicly shaking hands with the President of the International Association of Psychologists before the tomb of Freud.

The assumption made, in this kind of thinking, that we have a superstitious theology to escape from, is a denial of the Christian Revelation. The notion that eminent scientists move nearer to Christianity when they reluctantly concede their own ignorance (as yet) before the mysteries of mind, is a defiance of the true nature of the Christian Message. You cannot "move nearer to Christianity" by changing your mind about the ego or the id. All that this chapter has to say about the challenge of the supernatural goes to prove the enormity of this fallacy. "He who is not with me is against me."

It is appropriate now to define summarily some of the characteristics which mark the presentation of the Christian Message when the reality of the supernatural challenge is evaded. First of all, dilution of the gospel message is usually accompanied by an undue emphasis upon the historicity—as opposed to the transcendence—of the Christian Revelation. It cannot be too strongly asserted that Christianity is distinguished from all other religions by the rich factual records of God's entry into history. But if we lay exclusive emphasis upon the birth, teaching, crucifixion, and resurrection of Christ as past events in history, and neglect them as expressions of God's present Love for us, then we undoubtedly weaken the Christian challenge. The great doctrines of Incarnation, Atonement, and Redemption speak, not merely of the sinfulness of certain Jews in the first century A.D., but also of our sinfulness to-day. They will not allow us to think of the Crucifixion simply as a wicked deed perpetrated by other men at a distant point in the past: they declare that we ourselves are crucifying Christ to-day. They will not leave us to reflect upon the Resurrection merely as the proof of a certain prophet's divine inspiration, or even merely as evidence of that prophet's own divinity: they assert that death is conquered for us in our own day, that salvation is offered to us and to all men through an eternal self-sacrifice on the part of Divine Love.

An all-important function of the central doctrines of the Church is to ensure that we do not read the gospels merely as history which is past. It is comforting to read them as mere history, comforting to fix the central Christian revelation within the limits of that remote period twenty centuries ago. By thus fixing the Christian revelation at a distance, we are enabled to escape the shock which it ought to give us. We can thus ponder the gospel story in detachment, weighing the evidence for this particular miracle and for that, comparing one record with another in order to arrive at the Highest Common Factor of authentic fact. We are also able to consider carefully the connotations of Greek and Hebrew words, in the earliest versions of the Scriptures, which have taxed the brains of translators. Armed with the latest researches, we set the gospel story securely in its first-century environment, making due allowances for contemporary habits of thought and behaviour.

Now all this historical and etymological study is important. It is vital that scholarship within the Church in regard to the Church's own records should be as scrupulous and honest as secular scholarship is in history, philology, and the sciences. But this kind of study is for specialists—indeed it is for specialists who are fitted by temperament and arduous self-discipline for exercising the researcher's detachment in a field where detachment can be spiritually dangerous. It is very questionable whether Christians generally ought to be burdened with much of the detail which, by its very nature, tends to confine the Christian revelation within history, and thereby detracts attention from its compelling, immediate, and supra-temporal significance.

The Church in her wisdom long ago established the formulas which preserve the emphasis upon the supra-temporal challenge. It is ironical that thoughtless voices should be raised to-day, asserting that traditional doctrines are abstract and academic, too subtle and complex for ordinary men and women. It is doubly ironical that the same voices should urge continuous popular interpretation of the gospels from the point of view of the scientific historian. This is a topsy-turvy attitude. The emphasis that subjects the gospels in all their historicity to a microscopic scrutiny which blots out the eternal challenge is the emphasis for scholars of a particular kind. What ordinary men and women need, to illuminate the gospel story, is the clear emphasis upon traditional doctrines; for these doctrines make the eternal pattern clear and the personal challenge immediate. The traditional doctrines of Incarnation, Atonement, and Redemption safeguard the supernatural reality of the Christian Revelation, ensuring that it is not swallowed up in temporal historicity.

A second characteristic of Christian preaching and teaching which dilute the Christian Message is the frequency of exhortations to moral improvement by self-motivated endeavour. No Christian needs to be told that he cannot make himself into a full man by the force of his own unaided will. Nevertheless there is much preaching in our midst which implies that such self-improvement is possible. Once again, the call to moral striving towards the good life, when it is unaccompanied by the call to self-surrender and acceptance of grace, is a call which divests the Christian Message of its supernatural meaning. The call to the self to improve the self does not reach out to the supernatural. It intrudes nothing between the self and its temporal experience. But the call to self-surrender is an invitation to give the self to God, so that he may do the work of remaking: the call to accept grace is an invitation to receive something from God by which his work of remaking may be accomplished. Repentance, self-surrender, and grace; these words all turn the soul to God. This utter and total entanglement of the Christian moral message in the supernatural is precisely what distinguishes it from the secular code of ethics. The Christian moral message is summed up in the command to abandon the self to God—to share, in however ridiculously small a measure—the desolation and humiliation of self-giving supremely attained on the first Good Friday. The secular ethical message is summed up in the command to make an endless series of good New Year resolutions—to assert the self time after time in the tremendous triumph of turning over a new leaf.

Between self-assertion and self-abandonment there is a great deal of difference. There is no less a difference between the secular and the Christian call to the good life.

A third mark of Christian preaching and teaching which dilute the Christian Message is vagueness and confusion about the central doctrines so clearly proposed in the creeds. It is not surprising that this vagueness should appear. For we have seen that the central doctrines of the Church are one and all wholly supernatural in their emphasis, and any attempt to whittle down the supernatural basis of the Christian Message must inevitably blur the clarity of credal propositions. The attitude we are here investigating is seen in its most insidious form when it attempts to cloud man's reasoning by a fog of so-called "charity". The idea is cultivated in some quarters that any individual's declared attachment to a specific doctrine is an affront to all those who happen not to accept the doctrine. In the name of charity and tolerance we are discouraged from openly proclaiming any clearly formulable beliefs at all. And yet, and yet . . . even in the act of writing, one is conscious of a certain exaggeration; for the tolerance of the tolerationists has its breaking-point. In the non-Roman communions there are just a handful of propositions which the charitable Christian is at liberty to flaunt as essential bulwarks against superstition and non-sense; and these are precisely the propositions which mark our separation from the Roman Communion.

The idea that Christian charity chiefly consists in not expressing opinions with which other men may disagree is tenderly cherished in some quarters, but it is fatal to a rational faith. A rational faith is not content to reach out blindly to an utterly nebulous supernatural: it finds something in the supernatural which it can cling to, something which is exactly what it seeks; and it can go some way towards definition of what that something is. A rational faith is not content to grope in total obscurity before an utterly unknowable God; it recognizes qualities in God's nature and gifts in God's offering which are the very things that answer its deepest needs, and it can make shift with human language to define what these gifts and qualities are. In defining, faith dogmatizes, and doctrines are born. A profound and stable faith is a rational faith; and a rational faith is susceptible to intellectual description.

To turn the back on all doctrinal clarity is not only a sin; it is a sin against charity. For Christian charity itself demands the preservation for posterity of the faith, in all its illuminating richness, which past generations have handed on to us. To evade doctrinal clarity in the name of charity is thus an intolerable self-contradiction. It is true that profound experience of the Faith, profound spiritual insight, belongs to the person irrespective of his intellectual stature. But it is largely at the rational level of intellectual communication that the faith is transmitted from generation to generation. Charity thrives only alongside clarity—clarity of moral motive, clarity of purpose, and clarity of conviction. Purity of heart is just such clarity of motive and purpose. Integrity of personal conduct is wholly grounded in clarity of conviction.

We may therefore reject absolutely the idea that to cling to a clear doctrinal position is the mark of bigotry and intolerance, and the subsequent suggestion that such bigotry and intolerance are the worst of sins against the highest of virtues, without which whosoever liveth is counted dead before God. If the Christian learns self-surrender and achieves something of the peace that passes understanding as a result of an inner desolation and shame, he will not seek to preserve others from the same shame and desolation. This is only one of the many thoughts which show Christian charity to be a rigorous and virile virtue, far removed from sentimentality. Again, if the Christian has found in orthodox doctrinal clarity an anchorage for soul and intellect amid the seething and turbulent uncertainties of contemporary thinking, current codes of behaviour, and prevalent evaluations, charity will not allow him to keep this anchorage as a private possession.

One further point is worth making in this connection. The proposition that strict dogma is to be avoided as the mark of bigotry and the occasion of strife is itself a dogma. The doctrine which proclaims that doctrines are not to be treated too seriously must submit to the judgement passed upon doctrines in general. The logical result of accepting this doctrine is to leave us without any kind of anchorage at all. We are logically forbidden to press the doctrine that doctrines ought not to be pressed.

Our whole argument has gone to prove the utter necessity of doctrinal clarity. For we have seen that only in the traditional dogma of the Church is there any sure safeguard against evading the immediacy of the gospel message. Without the universalizing force of the doctrines of Incarnation, Atonement, and Redemption, the whole gospel story is pushed firmly back into a history from which we are comfortably remote and detached.

A fourth mark of Christian preaching and teaching which dilute the gospel message is neglect of the Church as a divinely established Body. Of course, the doctrine of the Church is likely to go the way of other doctrines when the rationality of the Christian Faith is blurred by sentiment, and the supernaturalism of the Faith is whittled away by materialism. For it is in the Church that Christian doctrine lives, in the Church that the Divine Incarnation survives as a supra-temporal fact. The weakening of the supernatural basis of the Christian Message is our especial concern here, and it is by a misreading of the significance of the Church that the supernatural involvement of Christianity can be most easily evaded.

If the Church is seen as an institution primarily devoted to humanitarian ends, then its true significance is neglected. If the Church is seen merely as a temporal institution preserving through the centuries the message of a great

Teacher and the code of behaviour which he recommended, then the real significance of the Church is evaded. Again, if the Church is regarded as an institution primarily devoted to the preservation in the human consciousness of a supreme pattern of the good life, then the Church is still misrepresented. Even though Christ's divinity be acknowledged and the gospels accepted in their fullness, the individual is still in error if he regards the Church as an enormous advertising agency, devoted to propagation of the greatest revelation of all time.

In the first place, the Church is a society; and its significance is that people belong to it—not, observe, that it teaches or preaches or heals or restores, but just that people belong to it. And, in the second place, the Church is a Divine Society, and its significance is that it is rooted in the supernatural. What does it mean to belong to a society which is rooted in the supernatural? Membership of such a society is plainly unlike membership of any purely earthly organization. It involves something more than just accepting a particular message and a particular set of rules and principles. It involves living with one's roots in another world. Where the Christian Message is plainly and honestly proclaimed, there will be no attempt to dilute or soften this utterly astonishing and shocking claim. If you live in membership of the Church, you live with your roots in another world. It follows that you will adopt criteria, standards, and regulations which may be absolutely incomprehensible to those who live wholly at the temporal level. You will be bound by a code which may be nonsensical to the materialist and to the pragmatist.

This truth ought to make a shattering impact. As an inheritor of the Kingdom of Heaven, caught in this middle world between life and death, you will live a double life. In many respects your ways will be no different from those of your respectable, unbelieving neighbours. Like them you will quite properly earn your living by honest toil, strive to feed, clothe, and house your family as bountifully as you can, and even seek to better your own earthly position by all just means. You will act as other good men act, pagan or Christian, when calls are made upon your charity and good-will. But, at the same time, the claims of another world will interpenetrate the claims of this; and there will be occasions when the former by-pass the latter. As a member of the Church, you will perform certain duties which can be shown, by earthly standards, to benefit no one. You will follow certain courses of conduct which are not in the least conducive to your earthly prosperity. You may submit to certain disciplines which are not necessarily even productive of better health. You will do many things, from day to day, for which there is, quite literally, no earthly reason. You will put yourself to great trouble over observances which do not, ostensibly, make a single poor man any the richer or a single ignorant man any the wiser, which give aesthetic pleasure to no one, intellectual enrichment to no one, political advantages to no one. You will do these things simply and solely because you are the member of a society rooted out of time. You will do them, to put it in familiar language, because you desire to love and worship God.

Any attempt, therefore, to seek continually for clear practical advantages for someone or other as a direct result of the Church's daily activity of prayer and worship, is plainly materialistic. The Church does not exist to do more cheaply and disinterestedly the work of social welfare which the State finds so costly. The Church is not primarily an institution for alleviating misery, removing poverty, healing the sick, or educating the young. All these are worthy causes. The Christian believes that he has a duty in regard to all of them: he is proud of the Church's record in humanitarian work. Moreover he believes that the Church achieves in this direction far more than mortal eyes can recognize, simply through the force of continual prayer. And the more the members of the Church, organized together, can do to remove poverty, suffering, misery, ignorance, and war, the better. But this does not alter the fact that in its essence the Church is a Divine Society whose existence is primarily justified by the fact that its members live by the light of another world.

The last mark of Christian preaching and teaching which dilute the Christian Message is the restriction of the Christian demand, especially in the intellectual sphere. This is the most difficult characteristic of diluted Christianity which we have to consider. It raises a vast subject, but a few comments must suffice at this point, for I have explored it in some detail elsewhere.[1]

The Christian challenge is a most comprehensive one. It demands that all experience and all thought take cognizance of the fact that the full life is entangled in the supernatural at the roots. Exactly in what way this demand must affect the activities of Christians in the intellectual, cultural, and educational spheres, has not been fully investigated as yet. There are many who feel that this investigation is long overdue, and that the need for it is one of the most pressing needs of our age. But one thing we can say with certainty: wherever in human thinking a judgement is made that reflects upon the nature of the human situation, then at that point a comment is called for in the light of the Chris an synthesis. If then a statement is made about the proper end of human life and about the satisfactions which it is proper for humanity to seek, that statement will be either true or false by reference to the Christian doctrines of man's nature and destiny. The same applies to statements about what it is

[1] See *Repair the Ruins, passim.*

proper for men to aspire to, to strive for, to fight for, to give themselves to. Judgements passed upon particular actions in the past and exhortations to particular courses of action in the future are alike susceptible to approval or disapproval from the Christian point of view. Analyses of the workings of the human mind, whether technical or imaginative, psychological or literary, can scarcely hope to be free of philosophical implications which can be judged true or false in the light of Christian doctrine. Again, any survey of human behaviour, which overtly or obscurely recommends certain habits, attitudes, or principles of conduct, can be treated as answerable to the morality of Christendom.

It is plain, from these examples, that in the study of such subjects as history, psychology, literature, art, educational theory, politics, and sociology, statements will continually be made which are grounded in certain philosophical presuppositions. And these presuppositions can be expressed as propositions, which will be either in consonance with Christian teaching or in conflict with it. No one will pretend that it is a simple matter to assess the judgements of specialist scholars from the Christian standpoint. No right-minded Christian will be so presumptuous as to suggest that his faith gives him the right to issue pontifical pronouncements upon matters on which he is slenderly or only moderately informed. That is why this is such a difficult matter to sum up. Its ramifications are enormous, and they extend wherever the human mind gives itself to intellectual study.

However, we are at least in a position to distinguish the attitude most likely to dilute the Christian Message. It is the attitude of assuming that Christianity has nothing to say to us which can affect our intellectual and cultural pursuits in general. It is the attitude which assumes that Christians are people who join in prayers and creeds on Sundays, and on Mondays, if they are intellectuals, betake themselves to studies which are no whit affected by their doctrinal allegiances. The assumption that Christians ought to agree only about a few limited propositions, which define the supernatural and establish rules for the good life, and which leave them floundering in absolute disagreement about everything else, is a defiance of the rational quality of the Christian Faith.

There is one invitation which the Church cannot extend to the historian, the scientist, the psychologist, the educationalist, the aesthete, and the philosopher. It is this: "Come over here and accept our creeds, and you can return to your studies as if nothing had happened." We do not need to read much in order to learn that there is determinism in the thinking of scientists and psychologists, unregenerate humanism in the thinking of aesthetes, educationalists, and sociologists, materialism in the thinking of economists and philosophers. Where there is determinism, materialism, or unregenerate humanism, there is heresy. Heresy is an ugly word with an ugly history: but then heresy is an ugly thing. It is a red rag to unlimited tolerationists and the sentimentalizers of diluted Christianity. But we must not be ashamed to resurrect the word. For if there is truth and orthodoxy, there is also error and heresy. It follows that any attempt to attain doctrinal clarity and stability will bring to light a mass of heresies underlying contemporary thinking. Every educated man feels the need to draw his intellectual knowledge into a synthesis which makes sense of his thought and his experience. Any educated Christian who examines some aspect of our current intellectual inheritance with this end in view, will inevitably meet with fundamental presuppositions which give a false account of man's nature and destiny. If he is honest, he will put his finger on such errors as he descries, and he must inevitably incur the obloquy specially reserved for heresy-hunters.

Nevertheless this work must be done. Mass education has brought such an enormous number of our contemporaries to the fringe of specialist knowledge in all kinds of subjects, that false presuppositions about life's meaning and man's vocation are spread more widely than perhaps ever before in Christendom. Possibly the major works of scholarship, by which the attack on these mass heresies must be guided, yet remain to be written. But in the meantime we do not lack the wisdom for distinguishing between materialism and supernaturalism, determinism and free will. And we can do our best to ensure that the intellectual comprehensiveness of the Christian synthesis is realized and explored.

Surveyal of contemporary movements in religious thought leads one to the conclusion that, in the near future, the dominating controversy within Christendom will be between those who give full weight to the supernatural reality at the heart of all Christian dogma, practice, and thought, and those who try to convert Christianity into a naturalistic religion by whittling away the reality and comprehensiveness of its supernatural basis. This conflict is already upon us and is pushing into the background controversies which caused deep and bitter strife in previous ages. The old controversies over grace and free will, faith and works, authority and individualism, are of course still with us; but they no longer in themselves represent the gravest disunity within Christendom. One reason for this change is that these controversies have now been so fully aired and so learnedly expounded that the educated Christian is in a position to see what were once mutually exclusive positions as differences of emphasis within a single coherent faith. Bitterly competitive doctrinal positions have become alternative emphases.

Thus a theologian like Reinhold Niebuhr, who puts the maximum emphasis upon grace and owes much to the Calvinist tradition, is not to-day accused by his opponents within Christendom of uttering nonsense, perverting the faith, and leading souls to perdition. Instead, his opponents point out that his excessive emphasis upon what is an essential Christian truth leads to an exaggeration. They will not deny that there is much of value to be learned from Niebuhr, but they will insist upon the necessity of taking contrary emphases into account. In the same way the opponents of so extreme a controversialist as Karl Barth do not generally charge him with the propagation of pernicious heresy of a diabolical kind. They are prepared to do justice to his assertions about the limitations of human reasoning and the powerlessness of the human will. Only they insist that his judgements must be balanced against those of Thomist thinkers who are schooled in Natural Theology and eager to reveal the rationality of the Christian Faith.

This change is symptomatic of a change in the temper of intellectual and spiritual life within the Church. That it betokens an enrichment of Christian charity we are most glad to believe. And it also indicates a willingness to learn from the sad lessons of history. But the change surely indicates something else too—a deep and growing awareness, sometimes fully conscious and articulate, at other times but dimly sensed, that a new and more menacing controversy is superseding the old divisions. This new controversy must have the primacy in our thoughts if we are to be fully in touch with the present situation in Christendom. It is a controversy more grave and momentous than those which it is superseding: the controversy between naturalism and supernaturalism, between a corroborating faith and a transfiguring faith.

Let us be honest with ourselves, analysing our response to the theological utterances of our day. As we read those thinkers who have gained a contemporary international reputation—Barth, Jaspers, Berdyaev, Niebuhr, Maritain,

Marcel—is not our disagreement over rivalries of doctrinal emphasis almost obliterated by a stupendous gratitude? Do we not mutter our thanks that, here again, the Christian Faith is presented to us surely and uncompromisingly as a religion of the supernatural? Are not other differences somehow swamped for us by the joy that another thinker, in this world corrupted by materialisms, is reaching firmly and squarely out of time, as the Christian should? In a situation of growing sensitiveness to the perils of trying to naturalize and secularize the Christian Faith, there is that within us which cries—"Anything, rather than that the Christian Message should be corrupted into a comfortable philosophy and code of ethics ornamenting a life hemmed in by finitude!"

We have reason to utter such a cry. It springs from a deep spiritual and rational rejection of an outrage against the Christian tradition. The outrage is being committed daily in our midst, wherever the supposed Christian Message is presented without reference to baptism, grace, and regeneration; without reference to Incarnation, Atonement, and Redemption; without reference to repentance, contrition, and self-surrender; without reference to the Church, the sacraments, and the Holy Spirit. That such emasculation of the Christian Message is possible is a shocking fact. That a "Christianity" can be popularized in which the fundamentals of Christian Faith, practice, and worship are annihilated, is an appalling testimony to our spiritual apathy and our theological illiteracy. If anyone argues that such emasculated "Christianity" is virtually non-existent, I can only reply that Providence must have seen fit to grant me a specially selected diet of "Christian" preaching and teaching, unique in its aberrations.

How has this corruption of the Christian Message come about? All we can say in answer is that the prevailing materialism of popular thought, so diversely represented in the attitudes and evaluations of the man in the street and his newspapers, has spread its infection so as to contaminate the only authority which brings a cure. The physician is himself afflicted with the disease.

Let us ask the more limited question: Why is there not in our intellectual and educational life a sufficiently virile Christian tradition to combat this virus? In striving to answer this question, one will perhaps stumble upon remedies for the disease, and therefore it is important to face it. Chief among the anti-Christian influences in our intellectual life is no doubt the much-advertised and much-lamented scientific bias of our culture. All that needs to be said about the dangers of allowing scientific and technological thinking to overlap their proper limits has been said more than once. We are aware now of this danger; and that is a most hopeful sign of the times. But is the prevalence of scientific thinking enough to explain the naturalization of Christian teaching within the ranks of those who call themselves Christian? Are there other reasons for the failure to realize the supernatural among the "Christian" leaders of our intellectual and educational thought?

It is only honest to voice the conjectures that experience breeds. One such conjecture is the familiar charge that our Public School system succeeds in inoculating the young against serious experience of the Christian Faith. We have learned enough from the psychologists to realize that inoculation of this kind may often achieve more damage than direct assault. It would appear that the Christianity of our Public Schools is inadequately rooted in the supernatural. We breed generations of men—leaders of men—who think they know what the Christian Faith is all about, though words like *grace*, *regeneration*, and *self-surrender* mean nothing to them. Theirs is a religion rooted in the pagan humanism of

Greece: Incarnation, Atonement, and Redemption are at best irrelevancies, at worst superstitions. Their code of moral conduct is high; but it is self-assertive rather than self-annihilating. Their values are cherished; but they are the Platonic values of intellectual, moral, and aesthetic endeavour, untransfigured by the eternal. For them the gospels are history and the Church a society devoted to the amelioration of moral and social life. Generalizations of this kind are always exaggerations; but they are needed to illuminate an obscure situation. It would seem that the Christianity on which many of our future intellectuals and leaders are nourished is seriously tainted with all those materialistic corruptions surveyed in this chapter, which dilute the supernatural element in the Christian Message.

Heavy charges are made here against the Public School tradition. No doubt there is plenty of evidence which could be produced to refute them. But it is equally true that a great deal of evidence could be produced to confirm them. The Public Schools are important in this connection precisely because they are officially Christian. As such, they minister to the health or to the disease of the Christian tradition in this country on a considerable scale. It is vital that, in so far as they teach and practise a professedly Christian Faith, it should be a Faith which the saints of the Church could recognize as their own.

The Public Schools, like so many of the traditional institutions of our country, bear testimony to the belief of our fathers that Christianity and civilization could hit it off together. There are perhaps many earnest and devout Christians to-day who would question the soundness of this view. If they were asked to support their conviction that the marriage of Christianity and civilization is an impossible dream, they would no doubt point to the secularized and eudemonistic "Christianity" of to-day as the result of attempting an impossible compromise. All Christians who believe that culture and civilization can be redeemed—and especially all who work in the world of intellect and education with this belief as their inspiration and justification— are burdened with the pre-eminent responsibility for ensuring that on their lips the Christian Message remains Christian. There are only two alternatives. Supernature will redeem Nature. Or Nature will seduce us to her service, like the harlot she is.

3

THE LANGUAGE
OF RELIGIOUS THOUGHT

IN ALL departments of human thought controversies arise because linguistic formulas are interpreted by different people in different ways. Conversely, men who are in substantial agreement with each other about a particular matter may be violently divided in the attempt to express their agreement in a common linguistic formula. Too many bitter controversies have arisen from divergencies of linguistic traditions, so that many thinkers have spoken of the intransigence of human language and its inadequacy to the task of expressing human thought. But perhaps we expect too much of language. Certainly the philosopher, in surveying the history of man's intellectual life, is more likely to be impressed by the community of connotations which language enshrines than by the alleged intransigence of this interpretative medium.

However that may be, it is impossible to join in discussion of the meaning of the Christian Faith without becoming involved in linguistic problems. There are many and acute reasons for demanding some account of the use of language in theological discourse, which will clear the air of confusions. For confusions there are in plenty. Controversy over the significance of the Book of Genesis turns largely on the interpretation which ought to be put upon words. The suggestion that Christian dogma, like the doctrines of the Trinity and the

Atonement, ought to be brought "up to date" is clearly one which asks for an inquiry into the exact nature of theological utterance. Suggestions that the creeds are archaic, and that the Church in her forms of worship is out of touch with the times, are plainly inspired by dissatisfaction with certain linguistic forms. Without listing any more examples, one can claim that the language of religious utterance raises crucial issues for many of our contemporaries. It may well be that apparent theological differences are façades covering linguistic confusion or misunderstanding. It may even be that Christian apologists are struggling to dispel theological ignorance when they might be more fruitfully occupied in attempting to dispel linguistic ignorance.

Contact with many who are stumbling on the fringes of intellectual acceptance of Christian truth does indeed suggest that this is the case. Christian doctrines are not generally rejected because they express unacceptable propositions: they are rejected because they are misunderstood. And the question of proper understanding is clearly in part a linguistic one. One is tempted to propose that no man ought to present the Christian Faith in intellectual terms to a mature audience without a preliminary discourse on the meaning of meaning. For whatever things are explored and understood by the men and women raised to literacy in our technological society, the nature of meaning is not among them. We must put alongside this uncomfortable truth the undeniable fact that the creeds and intellectual formulations of Christian belief are framed in such a way as to presuppose a considerable degree of linguistic sensitivity in those who use them.

The first important characteristic of language is that it is not an individual inheritance—like a man's own body—but a communal inheritance, like the civilization into which he is born. A man has rights over his own body which he certainly cannot claim over the language he speaks. If a man climbs a tree, he embarks upon a concentrated act in which the collected resources of his individuality are pitted against the objective world. But if a man resorts to verbal expression, he forsakes his individualness, entrusting himself to a medium whose significance lies wholly in the fact that it is *shared*. All meaning is a shared inheritance which resides in the communal human consciousness. That is why meanings have to be acquired by the individual slowly and laboriously in the early stages of his life. A child does not have to acquire a body from the community at large by submitting himself to the acceptance of certain established conventions; but he has to acquire meaning thus. Meaning is therefore a tradition, and it is a tradition with a very peculiar characteristic. For it survives by being preserved in the human consciousness, and at the same time it sustains that very consciousness which preserves it.

What keeps a word alive is the fact that large numbers of people agree in allowing to it a certain connotation. A word dies, as for instance the word *pelf* has died, when there is no longer a sufficient number of people for whom it carries a connotation. The presence of a word in the dictionary, in old books, and in the brains of a few scholars, is not of itself sufficient to justify us in speaking of the word as "living". A word is archaic, therefore, not because it connotes something out-of-date, something no longer seen or no longer believed in, like the words *centaur, witch, cannibalism, chariot, dryad, phoenix, toga*, or *gladiator*, but because it has a connotation which is generally not understood, like *codpiece, eale, greaves, pricksong*, or *fitchew*. This point will be important when we come to consider the allegation that liturgical formulas and doctrinal propositions are couched in archaic language. Meantime our concern is with the fact that meaning is a communal inheritance which cannot survive without communal acquiescence.

This does not imply, of course, that individuals cannot create meaning. They can both create it and change it. Some unknown individual gave the words *Iron Curtain* their present connotation: but the survival of the meaning carried by these words is guaranteed only by communal acquiescence.

Words are not, therefore, wholly at the service of the individual to do whatever he likes with them. A certain humility is required of men when face to face with any great tradition, and the tradition of language is no exception. Moreover a certain loyalty is required of individual men, when they presume to make use of an inheritance whose very survival depends upon communal loyalty. In other words, the individual has no right to weaken an inheritance which depends upon the support of all for its nourishment. He has every right to enrich the inheritance, if he can. But attempts at enrichment need to be disciplined, or they will fail of their purpose, and debilitate what they ought to nourish. This is the problem of poets especially, for poetry is the prime vehicle for the enrichment of meaning.

We may question whether those who use language for the purposes of Christian evangelism and theological controversy are sufficiently alive to the need for humility and loyalty to the linguistic tradition. Indeed it is probably true that religious controversies themselves generally bear witness to various degrees of disloyalty to the linguistic tradition. Now there are two notable ways of being disloyal to the linguistic tradition, and thus weakening, instead of supporting, the communal inheritance of meaning. One is the tendency to linguistic privatism—which excessively restricts the connotation of words, beyond the limits set by the communal tradition. The other is the tendency to linguistic dissipation —which excessively expands the connotation of words, beyond the limits set by the communal tradition.

It is necessary to quote examples of contemporary verbal

habits in order to illustrate this point. It is relevant to draw these examples from theological utterance. In doing so, I must emphasize that at present linguistic issues alone are under consideration: they are artificially separable from the theological issues raised by the illustrations. First an example of current linguistic privatism: Anglo-Catholics, brought up in a well-defined tradition of rigorous Churchmanship, have been known to speak in the following terms of members of the laity, members of the priesthood, and even members of the episcopacy, who happen to hold views more latitudinarian than their own: "So-and-so. Oh, he's a very good man—but not a Christian, of course." This means, in fact, that So-and-so puts too little emphasis upon the historic Apostolic Church, her priesthood and her sacraments, as channels of Grace; that So-and-so puts a Protestant emphasis upon the Bible as the sole ultimate authority in matters of doctrine; that So-and-so hammers away at the need for individual spiritual experience, whilst holding no brief for auricular confession. Whatever our views on the theological controversy represented by this kind of statement, we must try to concentrate solely on the linguistic aspect of this limitation of the word *Christian*. If we do so, we shall surely be compelled to admit that here is a case of quite unjustifiable linguistic privatism—of disloyalty to the linguistic tradition. Now it may be that we have the utmost sympathy with the speaker's theological point of view. It may be that we share his desire to see all Christians recognizing the authorities that he recognizes. But we must still oppose him on linguistic grounds. What you or I feel that the word *Christian* ought to mean is one thing. What the word does mean is another thing. And, for weal or woe, it embraces Roman Catholics and Plymouth Brethren. This is here stated, not primarily as a theological fact, but as a linguistic fact. Of course, we may wish to change the linguistic tradition. If we think clearly and strongly about anything at all, we are sure to wish to change it. Human thinking and human endeavour cannot be fruitful without such changes taking place. But a sense of linguistic responsibility, as well as a sense of theological responsibility, must accompany all attempts to influence word-meanings in the direction of greater restriction. This sense of responsibility is loyalty to the linguistic tradition. Violence to the linguistic tradition merely creates confusion—and to use words in the service of confusion, rather than in the service of clarity, is always unpardonable on linguistic grounds, however justifiable may be the theological motive behind it. Yet it is extremely difficult to make ardent controversialists responsive to this point. So many of them assume that a linguistic criticism is also necessarily a theological criticism.

It is right to give a corresponding example of the opposite tendency—towards dissipation of meaning by undue expansion of the recognized connotation. For this purpose we must look, not to the theological rigorists, whose fault is usually that of privatism, but to the latitudinarians, who are past masters in verbal dissipation. One has heard this kind of thing: "The Great Church is what I believe in and belong to, the real Catholic Church, the Universal Church—the community of all who want to serve their fellowmen, the society of all who strive towards a fuller knowledge of reality." On the same lines runs a notorious hymn:

> City of God, how broad and far
> Outspread thy walls sublime!
> The true thy chartered freemen are
> Of every age and clime.
>
> One holy Church, one army strong,
> One steadfast high intent . . .

Again, let us concentrate upon the linguistic issue. This is not what the word *Church* means. Of course, we have the right to wish it to change its meaning. And the poet is peculiarly privileged in making movements towards such change. One of the established conventions of poetry grants the poet especial liberty in this respect. We presuppose that a poet will make use of this peculiar freedom when we begin to read his verses. Perhaps therefore it is less fair to quote the hymn than to quote the prose statement. But they both testify to the popularity of a specific kind of disloyalty to the linguistic tradition. So much certainty exists about the connotation of the word *Church*—which is unquestionably more restricted than the connotation of the word *Christian*—that the linguistic tradition cannot be said to sanction a usage which turns the relationship topsy-turvy. If established word-meanings can be said to have any validity at all, we cannot claim that the beneficent materialist and the altruistic atheist belong to the Church, however Great. Claims for the freedom of individual thinking, broadmindedness, tolerance, and largeness of vision can be raised in defence of all kinds of private eccentricities; but they cannot excuse the blatant and perverse misuse of a word. Such claims, in a case like this may testify to charity. If so, well and good: but they also testify to illiteracy.

Disloyalty to the linguistic tradition, then, breeds controversy among Christians themselves. We must now turn to the much more momentous linguistic heresies which create confusion between believers and unbelievers. Chief among these heresies is the idea that a clear distinction can be drawn between the scientific and the metaphorical use of language. There is assumed to be a scientific vocabulary and usage which are concrete, precise, and so objective that they do not allow for the kind of misunderstanding which results from subjective bias in speaker and hearer. There is also supposed to be a metaphorical vocabulary and use of language which are abstract, vague, and ultimately un-reliable, because they put no limits upon variety of inter-pretation due to subjective bias. The scientific use of language is alleged to be exemplified in the works of natural scientists, psychologists, and sociologists. The metaphorical use of language is supposed to be exemplified in the writings of metaphysicians, theologians, and aesthetic specialists.

So much damage has been done to the intellectual climate by this theory that it must be accounted one of the two or three most pernicious heresies of our time. The idea that you are expressing meaning if you say "The Forth Bridge is *x* yards long", whilst you are merely making a meaningless noise if you say "God is Love", has now given birth to such a brood of subsidiary heresies about the nature of human thinking, that many years of patient linguistic instruction will be needed in order to repair the damage.

In the first place, we must recall that meaning is a traditional inheritance residing in the communal conscious-ness. This fact takes no immediate cognizance of the distinction between concrete and abstract words, between so-called scientific and so-called metaphorical expressions. The meaning of the words *square* and *house* resides where the meaning of the words *remedy* and *unity* resides. The meaning of the word *square* does not reside merely in the fact that we can point to a square drawn on paper. If we had no word *square* and no equivalent, so that we had to construct the unified meaning each time we wanted it, speaking of a *right-angled quadrilateral* (as we speak, in default of a single word, of a *right-angled triangle*), then the human consciousness would be the poorer, but the realm of objective actuality would be no different. It is in the human consciousness that this unified concept is comprehended as a whole so that a single term can express it. It is likewise in the human consciousness that the concept *remedy* exists as a single entity. He would be a fool who would claim that the meaning of the words *Iron Curtain* resides in metal and draperies.

This is not subjectivism; nor is it philosophical idealism. The theory that meaning resides in the human consciousness, in such a way as to allow equally for the validity of concrete and abstract terminology, can exist alongside a thoroughly realist attitude to the objective world. For meaning is an interpretation of that which we experience. Meaning continually throws us back upon our experience of the external world, and indeed it only exists by virtue of the reality of the external order. Words like *remedy*, *beauty*, and *love* work by their connection with our past experience—and with the past experience of humanity preserved in the communal consciousness—as surely as do words like *square*, *hand*, and *dynamite*. The claim made here is that we—and our ancestors—have experienced love as well as squares, beauty as well as hands. We claim that the inheritance of meaning handed on to us does justice to the past experience of mankind. We believe, in fact, that humanity has not been erring stupidly for centuries, in allowing language to grow which expresses experience other than that of direct sensuous contact with the tangible and the visible. It has not been reserved for the twentieth century to correct the linguistic fallacies of thousands of years of history. Our position is fundamentally realist. It accepts the reality of squares, hands, and beauty.

It should be noticed that there is one difficulty which the logical positivists and their numerous disciples in the theory of language have not faced. Suppose, as a hypothesis, that they established their case. Suppose, in short, that they proved in some way that we have no experience of anything except the phenomenal world as a physical construction appealing directly to the five senses. Suppose they proved that we have no right to speak of God, love, beauty, or spirit, because we have no experience of them—only subjective delusions based upon the superstitious inheritance embodied in our language. The scientific thinker must be scientific to the end. If this were proved, it would be proved only for our own day, only for our own generation. We should have every reason to doubt whether previous generations had not had experience, which we now lack, of supersensible and super-natural things no longer exposed to the human mind. Indeed, if the positivists did thus prove their case, they would *ipso facto* give the strongest evidence for believing that human experience had changed in just this way. If we establish that meaning is wholly derived from plainly ascertainable experience rooted in the phenomenal world, do we not imply that the men who created words like *God*, *angel*, *devil*, *soul*, *immortality*, and *heaven* had themselves plainly ascertainable experience of the things these words connote? Is not the immense legacy of "superstitious" language the surest evidence of experience corresponding to it? No true scientific thinker can afford to ignore evidence on this scale.

In fact, of course, the attempt to distinguish between a scientific and an emotive, metaphorical, or poetic use of language, is based upon a fallacy. The fallacy is that some words are metaphorical and therefore untrustworthy, whilst others have the character of pure labels and are devoid of poetic and associative undertones. But the research of philologists and semanticists reveals a metaphorical content in language wherever it turns its attention—in abstract and concrete words, in scientific and poetic words. Degrees of metaphorical content vary, it is true, but they do not vary in accordance with the distinction between scientific and non-scientific terminology. The word *apprehend*, a favourite with psychologists, has little poetic appeal, but it is a pure metaphor from the act of grasping physically. In Elizabethan days the verb was used of physical action. The officers of the law apprehended criminals. Now it is largely confined to the technical and scientific domain. The existence of the parallel metaphor, to *comprehend*, has enabled us to use one word for general purposes and to hand the other over to the specialist for his jargon. (And, of course, the existence of homelier words, like *grasp* and *seize*, reserved for physical processes, has enabled us to be lavish with the Latin derivatives.) Latinists do not need to be reminded of the high metaphorical content of such scientific terms as *gravity*, *relativity*, *impulse*, and *circumference*.

Owen Barfield has quoted the very instructive example of *focus*. *Focus* is a Latin word meaning *hearth*. Its first scientific use, in the eighteenth century, was a typical instance of the kind of creative poetic thinking which makes new meanings by a metaphorical process. A point is said to stand in relation to other points as the hearth stands in relation to those who sit around it, their gaze centred upon it, and themselves being united in relationship to this common centre. We no longer think about a hearth when we use the word *focus*, but the metaphor is crucial, none the less. Without the metaphorical process—essentially an act of the poetic imagination—the new meaning could not have come into existence. Science relies upon the poetic for the very vocabulary it employs— even for the vocabulary it employs for the purpose of decrying the poetic.

If, then, the vocabulary of philosophy, theology, and poetry is figuratively created, the vocabulary of science is equally so. The figurative content is as apparent in *focus* as it is in *spirit*. And the farther one traces back the history of words, the richer is the figurative content revealed. We know that the word *character* has developed, within the history of Western culture, from a Greek word meaning *an instrument for engraving*. We can trace its development—an engraved mark, a mark generally, a symbol, a feature of outward appearance, a trait marking the inward disposition, and so on. But this is not all. For if we trace back the Greek word outside the limits of our Western culture, we find that it derives from a word meaning *an instrument for making a furrow.* As so often, our researches lead us back, far back, to the primitive simplicities of husbanding Nature.

The discovery of Sanskrit has enabled scholars to trace back to common roots words which, in recognizably related forms, are current in several languages of the Indo-European family. It is to this family that the parent-languages, Teutonic (the ancestor of Anglo-Saxon) and Italic (the ancestor of Latin), belong. We are now in a position to take a view of linguistic development on an enormous historical scale. If words like *character* turn out to have grown by a metaphorical process, what of words which seem most like pure labels for objects in the natural order? Some of the evidence here is disputable, and there are controversies among the learned, but it seems clear that the metaphorical content of such words is equally prominent in the long view. Max Müller claimed that *serpent* is ultimately derived by a metaphorical process from a root meaning *to creep*, whilst the corresponding Latin word *anguis* is derived metaphorically from a root meaning *to throttle. Cave* is said, in origin, to mean *place of cover crow*; to derive from a Sanskrit root meaning *to sound thunder*; from a root meaning *to stretch*—the same root that gives us *tender, thin,* and *tone.* Such discoveries, attended though they are by conjectures, at least dispose for ever of the crude idea that language originates in a simple system of distributing labels to objects given to sensation.

Need we go so far back in order to appreciate how new meaning is created? If we could really reach the beginning, so much would be revealed that it would be necessary for every serious thinker to follow the path. As it is, we merely discover the same processes happening in apparently endless sequence that happen in our own day. *Thunder* turns out to be a centuries-old metaphor, where *Iron Curtain* is a metaphor of a few years ago. New meaning was undoubtedly created by the poetic act which gave us *Iron Curtain*; but the new meaning was rooted in the already known. Had it not been so rooted, it would have been nonsensical. The words sum up for the human consciousness a feature of contemporary European life which demanded to be organized as an intelligible concept. The organization was achieved by lifting the words *iron* and *curtain* from their established contexts and planting them together in a context to which previously they were in no way attached. This is metaphor; and all meaning is soaked in it.

We are now in a position to answer those who claim that religion uses language which is unreliably metaphorical. If it does, then so does science. The metaphorical element is common to all human utterance. The unreliability, in so far as it exists, is common to all human knowledge. The man who says, "I cannot believe in God, but I believe in a dynamic force behind the universe", is thus adopting a very peculiar position. The word *God* is personal. To posit a God is to assert that the first principle behind the created order is not inferior to the products of that order, of which man is one. It is to assert that the first principle transcends what is derivative from it by being at least equal in stature and capacity to the best of those derivatives. To posit a God is, in short, to claim that the first principle has at least those qualities of personality, rationality, and purpose which human beings glory in. There is nothing very irrational about this claim. It is odd that human beings, whilst admitting their own personal and rational qualities, should wish to describe the first principle of all things by a metaphor like *dynamic force* drawn from the science of physics. "I believe that the first cause is vastly inferior to the best of its effects: I believe that the first cause stands in relation to personality as the motion of a dynamo stands in relation to human willing." This is honest and tolerably clear; so that we can allow it to stand without further analysis. Of course it is nonsense.

"I cannot believe in your personal God, but I respect the Supreme Being whose impulse sustains the universe." Is this any better? What does it amount to, this rejection of a personal God in favour of a Supreme Being? Max Müller tells us that *being* is a metaphor from *breathing*. *To be* is *to breathe*: by an easy transference the former verb takes on a separate existence. The process of breathing is the physical mark of the distinction between the living and the dead. It is appropriate that it should have provided us with a word to characterize the process of existence, so difficult to define. If we deny that God is personal, we are left with two alternatives. Either God is a kind of animal, existing on the sensual plane without the exalting characters of reason, purpose, and self-consciousness. Or God is inanimate. One may take it that no one conceives of God as a depersonalized brute. We are left then with an inanimate thing which, when metaphors are rigorously purged, turns out to exercise the function of breathing. The Deity is nothing more than an automatic pair of bellows.

The purpose here is not to lay the foundations of a natural theology. Ours is a more modest task; to advertise the need for a linguistic approach which will help us with our controversies inside and outside the Church. As the failure to recognize that meaning is a shared inheritance confuses controversy between Christians, so the failure to recognize that meaning is a figurative inheritance confuses controversy between believers and unbelievers. We have the right to bring the soundest linguistic thinking to our aid in dissipating the appalling fog of intellectual error which darkens the lives of so many who form their opinions at second-hand. It is clear that, if the positivist denies us the word *spirit* on the grounds that it is a mere metaphor from *breath*, we have the right to deny him the verb *to be* on the grounds that it is a metaphor from *to breathe*. What difference can it possibly make that the one is an older metaphor than the other? No responsible thinker could allow that fact to count at all. If everything that *spirit* represents in the communal consciousness is a superstitious growth that reason cannot tolerate, then everything that *to be* represents comes in the same category. The positivist cannot be allowed to say "I am a positivist", but only, "A positivist breathes here". He may be satisfied with this. But he will get into grave difficulties in trying to correct, "Napoleon is dead".

It is time to consider the allegation that doctrinal propositions and liturgical forms of worship are couched in language which is archaic, out of touch with contemporary thought, and so forth. We have seen that a word is not archaic merely because it represents something which does not enter into the practical day-to-day experience of contemporaries—like *chariot, incubus, cannibalism,* or the verb *to scalp.* A word is archaic when it represents a meaning no longer alive in the communal human consciousness. To say that a word is archaic is to say that it is no longer meaningful for our contemporaries. But it is plain that the language of credal propositions and established forms of worship is still meaningful to the large majority of those who use it. It is, therefore, not archaic. Of course, it has existed for a long time. It brings with it the atmosphere of the past. And surely it ought to do so. The language of the Christian creeds would be false to the meaning if it contained only the atmosphere of the present. For the meaning has existed for a long time unchanged and unchangeable. It is absolutely essential that language which expresses a meaning packed with historic continuity should reflect this continuity. If it did not reflect this continuity, it would be false to its meaning: indeed, the meaning itself would be destroyed. For meaning, as we have seen, survives in language. A meaning which bestrides the centuries can be expressed only in a language which bestrides the centuries. This follows logically upon the fact that language expresses meaning.

The duty of Christians, in this matter, is to keep the meaning alive and to spread its permeation of the consciousness of their fellows. There is no attack upon language which is not an attack on meaning. It is a hard thing to say, and it must be said with humility, but the truth is this. The statement, "I find the language of the creeds archaic", can only mean, "The significance of the Christian Faith has not been embraced by my consciousness".

Behind misunderstandings on this point looms the fallacy that meaning is separable from the language which contains it. But since meaning is a tradition of the human consciousness, how is this tradition preserved and transmitted except in the words which express it? Destroy the words and you destroy the meaning. We have long learned that a prose paraphrase of a soliloquy in *Hamlet* cannot be said to convey the same meaning as the original poetry. If we lost the text of *Hamlet* and all memory of its lines, could we in any sense be said to preserve its meaning? Meaning is inseparably enshrined in words.

Perhaps it would be illuminating to press further the analogy between a great work of imaginative literature, like *Hamlet*, and the Christian creeds: for the status of the creeds in theology is, in some respects, not unlike the status of *Hamlet* in literature. In both literature and theology the whole body of interpretative criticism exists only so that, having encountered it, we can return to the established texts with new understanding and new insight. We do not study Shakespearean criticism in the hope that one day we may be in a position to rewrite *Hamlet* and *King Lear* in a phraseology more akin to the vocabulary of contemporary conversation. We study the critics in order to deepen our understanding of Shakespeare's poetry, and we are neither surprised nor disappointed when all the researches of the specialists and the explanations of the interpreters render the established texts more precious and sacred in our eyes. It is the same with the venerated formulations of Christian worship and profession. The more efficiently the Church does its work of teaching and interpretation, the more unwilling will Churchmen be to countenance any tampering with the text of the creeds, or even—on these grounds at any rate—with the text of established liturgies.[1]

We must not, of course, press too far the correspondence between the creeds and masterpieces of imaginative literature. For indeed no one can pretend that the language of the creeds is as remote from contemporary modes of thought as are the soliloquies in *Hamlet*. There is no linguistic difficulty facing the congregation at church on Sunday comparable to the linguistic difficulties facing the audience at the Old Vic on Saturday. This point is worth emphasizing, for would-be improvers of the creeds frequently claim that they are especially serving the interests of the "common man". The twentieth-century "common man" is notoriously hungry for education, and it may be doubted whether this is the right point in history for the Church to weaken its intellectual demand upon him.

It would be wrong to underestimate the intelligence of the

[1] This is not to deny that there may be sound *theological* and *liturgical* reasons for reforming our liturgies: but there are no sound *linguistic* reasons for so doing.

laity in this matter. It is one thing to claim that the public badly needs theological and linguistic instruction, and quite another thing to claim that they are generally incapable of responding to such instruction. Churchmen who protest that traditional theological phraseology is too difficult for twentieth-century parishioners, might do well to reflect upon the fact that thousands of humble men these days master specialized technological vocabularies with an ease embarrassing to the outsider. Can we even listen to the explanations of our garage mechanic or of the man from the radio shop without being shamefully dragged out of our depth? This is an age of enormously expanding technical vocabularies among our citizens generally. It is also an age of developing literary sensitivity. The popularity of the new poetic drama of T. S. Eliot, Christopher Fry, and others suggests a widespread, unsatisfied appetite for literature which, though superficially obdurate in its wording, rewards the attentive mind by the suggestiveness of its imagery and the richness of its symbolism. The language used in Christian worship is not as difficult as the vocabularies of the garage and the radio shop; and it is far easier than the vocabulary of the Mercury Theatre.

Of course there always are, and there always will be, those to whom technical vocabularies and rich imaginative literature are meaningless. But, as Dom Gregory Dix has so forcibly pointed out in *The Shape of the Liturgy*, the central form of worship in the Church, the Eucharist, is first and foremost an action in which all present play their part. Only secondarily is it a form of words. The acts of offering, consecration, and communion are so utterly simple that no man can claim failure of understanding as a reason for not taking part. If there is a set form of words at all, accompanying an action so frequently repeated, it must be one so rich in symbolism and so packed with history that every acquaintance with it but stretches the mind to new breadth of understanding.

Neither linguistic theory nor practical considerations will substantiate the demand for modernization of creeds and liturgies. We should rightly welcome any quantity of sound interpretation of Christian dogma which exploits the vocabulary and the environment of the contemporary world. We need such interpretation perhaps more desperately than it has ever been needed before. But we need it so that we can return to the recitation of our creeds with increased awareness of the comprehensive doctrines they proclaim.

Surely, however, it ought not to require any very elaborate argument in order to induce a Christian to pause before questioning the language of traditional theological utterance. Is not a certain humility required before language which has satisfied the greatest scholars and saints, not only of history, but also of our own age? Cannot the test of experience count for something here? Surely a man cannot read religious literature for long without discovering that those who have progressed, and do progress, furthest in the spiritual life and in the understanding of the Christian Faith, have found the traditional language of theology and liturgy ever more meaningful, comprehensive, and apt. We shall find no rebellion against the traditional language of the Christian Faith in the books, or on the lips, of those most fitted to comment, by the saintliness of their lives, the intensity of their spiritual experience, and the depth of their religious understanding.

We need go no further in this particular. Linguistic theory and living experience both point clearly to the same conclusion. If the language of doctrinal propositions and of liturgical forms is generally obsolete and irrelevant to our time, then the Christian Faith is itself obsolete and has no significance for our generation.

＊　　　　＊　　　　＊

The argument hitherto has gone to prove that the alleged difficulties encountered in the language of theology are not real difficulties—or, if they are real, that they are certainly not peculiar to theology. The problem of metaphor itself is no more a problem for theologians than it is, or should be, for scientists. But, nevertheless, there *is* a difficulty in theological language which is peculiar to theology. It has nothing to do with archaism or obsolescence. This peculiar difficulty must be investigated, because it is frequently the real difficulty disturbing people who imagine that they are upset by metaphor, allegory, or archaism. And the difficulty springs from the fact that the range of theology is wider than the range of any other science. Theology reaches out to embrace the eternal.

We must distinguish between three kinds of events, or truths, described by theological propositions. First of all, there are events which have been wholly contained in history, such as the birth of Christ at Bethlehem and the purely historical facts of Christ's ministry, the Last Supper, and the Crucifixion. Secondly, there are events, or truths, which have been partially contained in history. In a fashion these truths come to us as part of the ordinary historical sequence, but they are involved too, in a quite peculiar way, in a pattern of significant events which transcends the finite. Thus the doctrine of the Incarnation both proclaims a historical fact—the birth of Jesus—and an eternal fact, that Jesus is the Son of God, God made manifest in human form. The doctrine of the Redemption likewise proclaims historical facts—that Jesus was crucified and rose from the dead on the third day—and a fact transcending the finite order, namely that this sacrifice was a self-sacrifice on God's own part, redeeming men from the bondage of sin by the supreme act of self-giving Love. In the same way, the doctrine of the Church as the Body of Christ both bears witness to the historic institution deriving from the historic teaching of Our Lord and his disciples, and at the same time testifies to the living reality of the Church as a community of those regenerate by Baptism and claiming the eternal inheritance promised by God. Thirdly, theology speaks of events, or truths, which are scarcely contained at all in secular history. Such is the doctrine of the Trinity, viewed as a definition of God's nature. Such too are the doctrines of Heaven and Hell, of the Fall of the Angels, and of Satan as the tempter of mankind.

I am aware that this differentiation, like most such attempts at systematization, simplifies the question so far that it falsifies to some extent. This falsification is justifiable only if it leads to clearer thinking. For the Christian believes that history gives evidence of the doctrines of the Trinity, and of Heaven and Hell. The whole Christian Revelation is in a sense contained in history. That is what revelation means. The Holy Ghost is in history just as surely as the birth of Christ. But secular historians would, in many cases, deny this. And their very denial makes the crucial point clear. For theology has to make statements on many different levels. At one moment it declares the birth of Christ and the fact of the Sermon on the Mount, and no historian, I suppose, would question that these events are contained in history. At the next moment theology declares that Christ was Incarnate God; and straightaway the unbeliever denies, not the past existence of the person known as Jesus Christ, but the fact that he was God. And again, theology has to speak of the eternal existence of the co-inherent Persons of the Trinity. At this point, the unbeliever may protest that theology is a fantasy of hypothetical nonsense.

Now, of course, these distinctions are obvious from the very nature of Christianity. The Christian Church exists in time and out of time. The individual Christian has this characteristic, *qua* Christian, that he lives in time and out of time; that he eats, drinks, and makes merry with other men, and at the same time strives to pattern his life to the demands of the Eternal. To do the Will of God is the law of the Christian life; and to do the Will of God on earth is to direct terrestrial life by an impulse and purpose which utterly transcend the temporal. It is to live with the soul alert to the impulses of the Infinite, with the will adjusted to the fact that man's vocation is to another life than this.

Every powerful attempt to weaken Christianity will take the form of an attack upon the supernatural in which it is grounded. Unbelievers, even aggressive unbelievers, do not generally attack the Christian ethic, as summed up in Christ's moral instruction. Rather they patronize it, and very often claim to observe it better than Christians themselves. Nor do unbelievers generally attack the veracity of the records of Christ's humanitarian work among the sick, of his exhortations to brotherly love, of his betrayal, trial, and death upon the Cross. What they attack is the impingement of the supernatural upon the natural—the fact that Christ was God, that the miracles were miracles, that the Church has any significance other than the significance of a brotherhood devoted to earthly ends. We cannot remain Christians and surrender the supernatural. In the impingement of the supernatural upon the natural lies the *raison d'être* of the Christian Faith. We should therefore be on our guard against all attempts to whittle away the supernatural. They will come in many guises: in the attempt to weed out all taint of supernatural intervention from the accounts of the miracles; in the attempt to emphasize Christ's significance as teacher, humanitarian, political rebel, or philosopher—anything but his significance as Incarnate God. We must expect the Church to be attacked for not being what it never pretends to be—an instrument wholly devoted to social welfare. Above all, we must expect attacks upon the language of theology when it pays attention to that which is essentially and supremely the concern of theology—the supernatural.

Any criticism which questions the right of theology to make statements about the supernatural, any criticism which doubts the rational validity of statements about the supernatural, any criticism which hints that traditional orthodox theological propositions about the supernatural are likely to be archaic and obsolete, touched with superstitions which twentieth-century enlightenment cannot endure, and any criticism which implies that theological propositions would be better reinterpreted in the jargon of current psychology and sociology—these are, each and all, expressions of the naturalistic revolt against the supernatural, of which our age is guilty.

Now the fact that theology makes statements on many different planes, with varying degrees of reference to the supernatural, makes it possible for the theologian himself to nourish a naturalistic bias. It enables a man to pursue so-called theological studies with zeal and persistence, whilst preserving an anti-theological suspicion of the supernatural, which in reality unfits him for theological study. This situation presents us with the spectacle of the untheological theologian, which is one of the curses of our time. This is the spectacle of the professional theologian who devotes himself exclusively to the study of that part of theological data which is wholly contained within history. To the investigation of this data he brings an acute historic perception, a comprehensive capacity for philosophical judgement and a thorough linguistic and etymological equipment. He also brings the naturalist's prejudice against the supernatural which makes true theological thinking impossible for him. He thinks he is a theologian, when in fact he is a historian and an etymologist. For it is the supernatural vision which makes theology theology. Without this vision it is merely history, psychology, or sociology. No amount of argument about the proofs of the Resurrection narrative can transmute this piece of historical research into theological utterance. The true theological vision, whilst maintaining the historical foundations of the revelation, lifts it at the same time out of history. The theological vision is the supra-temporal vision which adds to the historical facts of Christ's Crucifixion and Resurrection the supernatural facts of Redemption and Atonement, as real now as they were two thousand years ago. It is the supernatural vision which transmutes history into theology.

Divinity courses in educational institutions are often almost wholly given up to the kind of untheological "theology" which we have been describing. The data from which theological thinking starts are painstakingly examined from a historical and etymological point of view. Unfortunately there it stops. The theological thinking never does start. The very subject which ought to bring before students the challenge of the supernatural merely nourishes their superficial approach to all experience at the historical and scientific level. The very subject which ought to give them a supra-temporal vision of the human situation bogs them down more firmly in the temporal. In theology the supernatural ought always to be the dominating fact; but it is treated as an embarrassing by-product of human speculation in the pre-psychological era.

Christianity suffers enormously from well-meaning but uninformed desupernaturalizers of the Christian revelation. And intellectual reluctance before the supernatural is in a very large measure due to a theological illiteracy which is embarrassed by propositions about the supernatural. Now it would be absurd, presumptuous, and misleading to give the impression that the language of theology has not been scrutinized to the last detail by theologians themselves. In fact the rational justification for the use of words to express the infinite truths of the Christian Faith has been examined with the utmost care. The quality of meaning conveyed by statements about the nature of God, for instance, has been rigorously scrutinized. And the limits of human capacity in describing realities beyond the finite have been defined for all time. Almost everything that needs to be said on this difficult subject was said by St Thomas Aquinas in his discussion of analogical statement and its validity as an expression of human knowledge. The first point to be emphasized, therefore, is a point which in the study of any subject other than theology would be taken for granted by all beginners: namely that the experts have investigated the question of theological language and have established the validity of theological utterance.

It is necessary to say this, because it appears to be believed in many circles to-day that, whereas there is an orthodox body of knowledge, corroborated by the experts, in every other subject of study, in theology there is only a mass of capricious conjectures, from which everyone is at liberty to choose what he wants to accept. If beginners approached mathematics as they often approach theology, they would, in the earliest stages as untutored fledglings, decide to accept the quadratic equation as valid and reject the logarithm tables outright as a piece of formalized superstition. They would pick and choose among the theorems of Euclid, accepting this and rejecting that, in blind ignorance of the fact that each is dependent upon the other. There are people who will gladly meet to learn astronomy or physics; who will cheerfully come together to be told which novels are good and which are bad—where they ought to have opinions of their own. They will assemble to *learn* literature, music, history, or biology. But they will not willingly assemble to *learn* theology. They assemble to discuss it—even, alas, to formulate it.

It would be out of place to attempt here to restate Aquinas's doctrine of Analogy. Anyone who wants to understand it can read Aquinas or, say, E. L. Mascall's *Existence and Analogy*. The point to be made here is that theology has faced up to the fact that it is theology—that it has to speak of the mysteries of the eternal. It has made its propositions after facing this fact fairly and squarely. It remains for us to consider the results. But we may reasonably tackle one limited question. Bearing in mind all we have said about the relationship of word to meaning and about the survival of meaning in the human consciousness, need we have *a priori* reservations about propositions defining infinite realities?

Meaning survives verbally in the human consciousness. It sums up the experience of our ancestors—those elements of experience which they were able to assemble in conceptual form through the medium of language. This is true of meaning of all kinds. Let us consider four statements:

1. *Apples grow on trees.*
2. *Prevention is better than cure.*
3. *Christ was the Son of God.*
4. *God is Love.*

Each of these statements is bred of human experience, and in each case the experience is rooted in the historical order and in scnsc-pcrccption. The first statement is plainly rooted in experience of the natural order. The second is rooted in repeated concrete experiences of many kinds—experience of disease, of criminal acts and the like. The third statement is rooted in a historical event recorded like other historical events, with more than the average amount of evidence to support it. The fourth statement is likewise rooted in historic experience by the fact that the Christ of Statement 3 uttered the proposition. In all these cases, then, the statement is the fruit of human experience of a sensuous kind and interpretation of it. Men have observed apples growing on trees and have seen epidemics halted. Men saw and heard that Christ was the Son of God, and heard him whom they supremely trusted declare that God is Love.

Suppose we wish to test the truth of these statements. On a strictly scientific basis only statement 1 can be verified. This is obvious. Statement 1 is a scientific statement in that it is a fact derived from observation of the phenomenal world, a truth abstracted from a multiplicity of identical instances. Statement 2 can scarcely be verified in the same way. It defies scientific experiment; and so it should, because it is not a statement of the scientific order. It is doubtful whether any apparent instance of prevention could be reliably proved to be such. Whatever is said to have prevented the development of a disease or the commission of a crime, can we be certain that, without this preventative, the disease would have developed or the crime been committed? That kind of certainty eludes us here. But there is rational certainty behind the statement none the less.

In other words, certainty dwells in some other criteria than verifiability by scientific experiment. Statement 2 represents a truth dwelling in the human consciousness, but this truth is not linked to the world of sense experience in quite the same way as Statement 1 is linked to that world. It is therefore not susceptible to the kind of testing to which Statement 1 may justifiably be submitted. Indeed we can link Statement 3 to the world of sense experience by a more fool-proof "scientific" connection than we can grant to Statement 2. For historical records exist, and there is a scientific way of establishing the authenticity of such records. This may be said to be only approximately fool-proof, in the way that the verdicts of juries are not infallible. But there is something more satisfactory to the scientific mind in pointing to a historical record, than in pointing to a man in a laboratory who has been prevented from having influenza.

The truth of a statement is tested by a technique appropriate to the category of thought to which the statement belongs. We do not regard generalizations like Statement 2 as suspect just because they happen to be scientifically unverifiable. Theological statements are tested by their consonance with historical fact and by their validity before the bar of reason. They depend upon a threefold foundation in experience, reason, and revelation. And, of course, accepted truths interlock with each other in mutual interdependence in the science of theology as they do in the science of physics.

We have established that for a statement to be true it is not necessary that it should be demonstrably so by laboratory experiment. Nor need it be verifiable by direct observation—or we should know nothing of history, which is no longer observable. Certainty is established in different modes appropriate to the category of knowledge to which the statement belongs. The propositions of orthodox Christian theology are guaranteed by an epistemological theory as rigorous and coherent as that of any branch of study. To pick and choose here is as much the mark of stupidity as it is in any other science. The certainty of the doctrine of the Trinity cannot be questioned without repercussions which upset the whole body of knowledge. To question this doctrine is to question the truth of Christ's words and of the apostles' and evangelists' teaching. It is therefore to question the reliability of the Gospels and of the Church's tradition. It will lead, like any other questioning of a central doctrine, step by step to the destruction of faith.

The most crucial question now arises. Since the propositions which refer to events not contained within the historical order are so closely interlocked with the propositions which refer to that which is contained in history, there can be no question of degrees of certainty in respect of the central doctrines of Christianity. This is the logical conclusion of our argument. The doctrine of the Trinity is not less certain than the facts of the Crucifixion. The promise of the Kingdom of Heaven is not less certain than the fact of Christ's birth in Bethlehem. Is there, therefore, no place for intellectual humility before the Eternal—for the humility of confessing that human knowledge is limited and the human vision is imperfect?

There is a place for such humility, of course. And it is where we ought always to have looked for it—in human language. Language as the expression of meaning is itself nourished upon human experience. Human experience is dominated for most people for most of the time by the facts of physical existence in the temporal order. Language reflects the limitations of this existence. As we should expect it to be, language is perfectly equal to the task of describing that which has occurred in time—in history. Language is perfectly at home in describing historical events such as it is daily practised in describing. It is less adequate to the task of describing that which is only partially contained in the temporal order—the fact of the Virgin Birth, the mystery of the Incarnation. It is least adequate of all to the task of describing that which, in terms of daily human experience, seems to be wholly other—ineffably exalted above the finite.

But this inadequacy of theological language is not measured by the adequacy of scientific utterance. Indeed the adequacy of scientific utterance is itself widely questioned nowadays by the scientists themselves. The inadequacy of theological language is the inadequacy of the finite to comprehend the infinite. There is no standard of adequate human expression by which to measure this inadequacy. Its only measure is the very infinity to which it reaches out. It is, in short, inadequate before God. But God probably does not need it. And for men we must believe it to be adequate in practice, for it is the language vouchsafed to us.

Theological truths are certainties for man. They do not vary in comparative certainty. They vary in the extent to which human language can do justice to them. This is not variation in certainty, and it is not therefore reflected in various degrees of credulity, confidence, or faith. It is a variation in human capacity and is properly reflected in various degrees of humility and self-abasement.

This, then, is the only proper reply to those who, whilst accepting a large part of Christian teaching as true, feel grave difficulties about accepting such doctrines as the Fall of the Angels and the Fall of Man. These doctrines interlock with the rest of Christian teaching so tightly and inevitably that a rational analysis of the Christian Faith renders it unthinkable to separate them in a special category of doubtful hypotheses. The element of unverifiability in these doctrines is quantitatively high; but this element of unverifiability is present in some degree wherever statements are made about the supernatural. And the involvement of the supernatural in the facts which constitute the Christian revelation is so all-pervasive that the believer must adopt a positive attitude of acceptance towards it. If this acceptance seems to get progressively weaker as we turn from the doctrine of the Resurrection to that of the Virgin Birth, and from the doctrine of the Incarnation to that of the Fall of Man, then there is something wrong with our attitude. We are allowing the demand for verifiability to raise its head. And what reason have we for allowing this demand to raise its head at some arbitrary point in the mid-course of theorizing? Logically speaking, we must either allow the demand for verifiability to dominate from the start, in which case the acceptance of the supernatural is wholly impossible; or we must abandon the principle of verifiability as the governing category in our thinking. And, in this case, the Christian Faith can be accepted as a whole.

As we proceed, then, from the doctrine of the Resurrection to that of the Virgin Birth, and from the doctrine of the Incarnation to that of the Fall of Man, our attitude should be modified, not by increasing doubt or incredulity, but by increasing humility and increasing awareness of human littleness and ignorance. That is to say, we admit the increasing inability of human utterance to do full justice to the truths which it is expressing. Unless this variation is seen as something other than a variation in certainty, our faith will not be sound. Provided, in fact, that the difficulty of the articles which set forward doctrines of the infinite, is seen to be primarily and essentially a linguistic difficulty, all will be well.

It is worth remarking here that the temper of the 1950s is not the same, in this matter, as was the temper of the 1920s or the 1900s. I am referring now to the younger generation. Christian teachers, brought up in an outmoded climate of opinion, are likely to misjudge the temper of to-day. So many of us were brought up at a time when the real intellectual difficulty of Christians was precisely the question of where to fix the arbitrary limit between acceptable doctrines and doctrines which seemed to ask too much of the human intellect. In short, the difficulty of previous generations arose at the point where the link with the phenomenal world seemed to be snapping completely—at the point of such doctrines as the Virgin Birth and the Fall of Man. Christian teachers who now make much ado over these "difficulties" before the younger generation are out of touch with the climate of opinion of their pupils.

Experience compels one to this point of view. For the

Christian teacher to-day rarely meets with the young man who accepts the Resurrection and draws the line at the Virgin Birth. It is an ironical experience, therefore, to come up against old men and men well advanced in middle age who speak cautiously and forebodingly of the doctrine of the Virgin Birth as though it were the supreme difficulty for the modern young man. The inquiring young man of to-day, who thinks for himself, has a difficulty of another kind—the difficulty of making a start. Once he has satisfied himself of the existence of God and the prevenience of supernature in the finite order, he will not of his own accord set arbitrary limits to what is acceptable in Christian doctrine. The young of to-day are looking for complete systems. Hence the appeal of Marxism and Jehovah's Witnesses. Hence too, we may admit, the resùrgence of Thomism as a living influence upon the young. Many of us believe that the temper of the young intellect to-day is healthier than that of pre-war generations. There is more whole-heartedness and a freer recognition of the scope of the rational. That is why it is the scepticism of St Thomas Aquinas that is relevant, not the scepticism of Victorians and Edwardians, vainly trying to adjust the claims of science and religion at a point midway between the Resurrection and the Incarnation. "Give us the Resurrection, so well authenticated by the canons of scientific history, and we will surrender the Virgin Birth as an unscientific hypothesis." This kind of attitude, on the part of religious teachers, is not only irrational but also irrelevant—hopelessly and ludicrously out of date. The young clamour for a system—whole-hearted, rational, coherent, and demanding an act of faith. The picking and choosing of liberal protestantism means nothing except to those brought up to it. The one thing we can most safely and certainly say of modernism is that it is no longer modern.

You will find among the young to-day an earnest

responsiveness to the scepticism of Thomas Hardy, precisely because it is logical and rooted in experience. And this is the kind of scepticism for which Aquinas caters. You will find no such responsiveness to the scepticism of Bishop Barnes. To a generation of people ready to pledge their souls in communist cells, or to knock at doors to proclaim an imminent theocratic world-order, such scepticism is neither here nor there. And this fact puts a peculiar responsibility upon the Anglican Church. The need is pre-eminently for a wholesale and rational dogma rooted in the supernatural. Those Christians have hit the nail upon the head who have pointed out in the religious press that even the old distinction between High Church and Low Church, Catholic and Evangelical, is disappearing before another more momentous distinction —the distinction between those Churchmen who accept the Christian Faith in all its supernaturalism, and those who try to whittle away the supernatural challenge and significance of Christianity. The spectacle in the educational world at present is often both ludicrous and tragic. It is the spectacle of Christian teachers apologetically minimizing that doctrinal content of supernatural Christianity for which the souls and intellects of their pupils are urgently clamouring. It is the spectacle of Christian teachers laboriously tussling over the chronology and authenticity of different gospel narratives before pupils who long to know only what the Christian Message is, what the Church has to teach. It is, in fact, what others have discerned it to be, the spectacle of Christian teachers inoculating their charges against the danger of incurring a potent dose of Christianity.

Unless we realize that modernism is absolutely and utterly out of date, that it caters pathetically for a historical phase that finally disappeared with the coming of the Second World War, we shall fail to rise to a most exciting opportunity. As evidence of the antiquity of modernism, we may point to the kind of Christian literature which has made the biggest impression of late years. At the most scholarly level, we may point to the books of Kierkegaard, Barth, Maritain, Berdyaev, and Brunner. On what Christian scholar's lips are these names not heard—and the names of Jaspers, Marcel, A. E. Taylor, and Christopher Dawson? Footnotes in Christian literature bring us back time and again to names like these. And if there is one thing to which all these thinkers testify, it is to the overriding reality of the super-natural and the futility of pseudo-scientific modernism. Again, at the more popular level, the works of G. K. Chesterton, C. S. Lewis, Ronald Knox, and Dorothy Sayers have attained enormous popularity, precisely because of their doctrinal clarity and whole-heartedness. Who nowadays reads Bishop Barnes? Where is the young man who quotes Julian Huxley's *Religion without Revelation*? The young intellectuals have other authorities than these, religious or anti-religious. It may be Kierkegaard, it may be Aldous Huxley; it may be Sartre or Buber, Solovyev or Maritain—but these are not the names of men who apologize for the supernatural or dilute religion to humanitarianism. And, lastly, the Christian men of letters whose message has really impressed this generation are those who have presented the impact of the supernatural upon the natural in its intensest form—T. S. Eliot, Gerard Manley Hopkins, Graham Greene, and Charles Williams.

There is too much force of sheer authority, sheer intel-lectual authority, behind whole-hearted supernaturalism for the modern young student to experience the doubts of forty years ago. That is, provided that we of an earlier and less rational generation do not indoctrinate him with the infidelities of our narrower vision. That we tend to do so cannot be denied. To young people crying out for the redeeming grace of God and the hope of the gospel promise we have the effrontery and presumption to offer discourses on the relative authenticity of various miracles and ingenious ventures into Greek and Hebrew etymology, which take the supernatural sting out of ethic and prophecy.

Which brings us back to the subject of language. As an approach to the problem of theological utterance, the kind of learned antiquarianism which dilutes doctrine and miracle by explaining away the supernatural potency of key words in Bible and Creed—this technique likewise belongs to a period of piecemeal scepticism that is happily ended. The temper of to-day, with its promise of wholesale scepticism or wholesale faith, demands rather that language itself should be justified. This justification must be provided. The meaning of meaning must be illuminated. The validity of theological statement and scientific statement must be inquired into. Above all we must present meaning as a shared inheritance of the human consciousness—a traditional legacy which grants understanding to us, and which we, in our turn, are called upon to enrich by new insights. The very nature of meaning is such that the stripping from a word of all its undertones and associations gathered during the Christian era cannot be accounted a necessarily edifying or clarifying procedure. Except for the specialist scholar, it is a process rather of confusing and falsifying. The meaning of a word is *not* the meaning of its ancestor of two thousand years ago. Unless we recognize that fact, we are unfitted to expatiate on the meaning of Biblical language. Yet it is odd that those Christians who are most anxious to see human thought progressing always to fuller understanding of reality, should themselves so often try to annihilate the enrichment of language which two thousand years of Christian experience have quite properly brought about. At one and the same time, they wish to grant the maximum of significance to changes and developments of human thinking, and to insist that what a Greek word meant over two thousand years ago, its derivative must mean to-day.

But meaning grows. Has not the word *spirit* been enriched during the last thousand years? Can we not see such enrichment taking place before our eyes? Is the word *freedom* quite the same since Berdyaev, the word *Incarnation* since Charles Williams, the word *despair* since Kierkegaard? The surest sign that religious thought is vital and profound will be the enrichment of the Christian vocabulary by new qualities of meaning. Thinking which enriches meaning is *ipso facto* creative. Thinking which succeeds in dissipating or annihilating meaning is always *ipso facto* moribund and unconstructive. In these two sentences there is much food for thought.

4

THE DRAG OF NATURE

THE PATH of a writer who chooses to attack a falsehood is safe and straight; but the path of a writer who sets out to correct a misleading emphasis is hedged about with traps and pitfalls. For instance, it is almost impossible to declare with fervour that schools ought to teach more Greek and Latin, without being accused by someone of making an attack upon the sciences. Nowhere is this perverse reaction more frequent than in the field of religious argument and exhortation. If you praise life-long chastity, you will almost certainly be accused of making an attack upon the married state.

The only defence against such misrepresentation is the power of logic. A man does not prove himself a teetotaller by inveighing against the evils of drunkenness. A husband might rebuke his wife vehemently for getting out the car in order to go to the butcher's shop two hundred yards away, to purchase a pound of sausages. But you could not prove, on this evidence, either that he disliked sausages or that he regretted the invention of the internal combustion engine. Nor could you justifiably conclude that he was a vegetarian or an opponent of free enterprise. Still less could you argue that he was possessed of a fanatical passion for physical exercise which led him to impose a sadistically spartan code on the members of his family.

The nature of the Christian Message is such that we need

to be especially on our guard against such exaggeration and misrepresentation on the part of those who do not see eye to eye with us. You can scarcely hope to plead for renewed emphasis upon a neglected aspect of the Christian Faith without laying yourself open to the charge of depreciating some other aspect. You cannot put a special emphasis upon grace without laying yourself open to the charge of undervaluing freewill. You cannot put a special emphasis upon faith without provoking the criticism that you are depreciating good works. The writer would seem to have no security from these counter-charges unless he makes his book a complete summary of the Christian Faith in all its aspects. Yet the risk must be run; for the work of renewing neglected emphases is necessary and salutary. And not all theological books ought to try to reproduce the balance and comprehensiveness of the creeds.

It seems desirable to issue this *caveat* in introducing a chapter which is concerned with the hostility of the natural to the supernatural, for of course the existence of this hostility is only half the story. The natural is friendly to the supernatural on so many counts that it may perhaps be thought perverse to spotlight the opposition between the two. But surely, in twentieth-century Christendom, there is small need to plead the case of the natural order. Indeed the case for Nature is always implicit even in a theological attack upon her corrupting influence. For a writer cannot criticize the limitations of naturalism without using in the process the hands, eyes and brains of natural man. To kneel in prayer, to sing in worship, to preach in exhortation—these are activities which involve the use of the limbs and the senses. We can have no experience of the supernatural, and make no deference to the supernatural, except through the activities of our physical bodies. We consume time and make movements in space as we declare the limitations of finitude.

Not even the crucifier of the flesh can attain to pure spirituality in this life in time. The monk who lashes his own back has to use his arms to do so.

No subtleties are needed in order to stress the dignity of the natural order and the exalted rôle we are invited to play in it. The gospels and the Acts, which form the basis of our faith, are not stories of disembodied spirits set in a vacuous infinity. They are records of men and women, with bodies like our own, who worked and travelled and preached within the historical sequence which now contains our own lives. Our Lord himself thought human bodies worth feeding and healing. He praised the flowers and enriched the festivities of a wedding-feast. He used the fruits of Nature and of man's handiwork in establishing a permanent sacrament of sacrifice and fellowship. He even rode upon an ass. It was devilry which sent the swine rushing headlong into the sea.

Why, then, is it necessary to speak of Nature's hostility to the Faith of Christ? Because he told us that his kingdom is not of this world. This was a warning—a warning which presupposed the temptation to try to make his kingdom of this world. In short, there was a paradox from the start—a combination of conflicting emphases which the Church can never escape. Indeed, the whole history of the Church is fraught with practical and intellectual conflicts and divisions over the problem of the relationship between the natural and the supernatural. Through long centuries of hard thought and living experience the Church has thrashed out a theology which reconciles these conflicting emphases. But there is always the danger, and there always will be the danger, that the fine balance of her Message will be upset, now this way and now that, as her sons struggle with the immediate problems of their own day.

Continual correction of theological emphasis is our only intellectual safeguard. Our problems are not new. They were implicit in the Divine decision to take on the life of the flesh, perhaps even in the Divine decision to create a temporal universe. They have therefore been well aired; and it is our business to make ourselves acquainted with the rich theological tradition which has given them their airing. We need to think theologically about every aspect of contemporary life and thought.

Indeed, it has always seemed to me remarkable, in these days of mass popular hunger for education, that the Church's offering in this connection has been so little regarded. There is a traditional Christian theology which the Church teaches—or rather, ought to be teaching—free gratis week by week; and if a man imbibes this teaching from his youth onwards, and then turns to survey his own experience by the illumination it provides, he will discover that he is a philosopher. And since philosophy in the universities sickened of the diseases of the age, the Church alone has preserved a healthy philosophical tradition. On the purely intellectual level, the insights she offers are such as to make the educative value of pseudo-philosophical evening courses in social studies and the like look meagre indeed.

We have been too shy of the rich intellectual inheritance handed down to us in Christian theology. We have neglected the illimitable relevance of our doctrinal tradition. Now we are beginning to pay the price of neglect, when any appeal to altruism, good-fellowship, or humanitarian sentiment can pass itself off as a specifically Christian exhortation. At this point one is tempted to pay a left-handed tribute to the overworked clergy of our country. Considering the vast amount of nonsense that one encounters daily on the pens and lips of those who address the public on secular matters in the press and over the air, it is quite astonishing that one so rarely finds anything other than good sound sense uttered in the pulpit. What is so disturbing, however, is that this good sense is sometimes but tenuously related to the fundamentals of the Christian Faith, if it is related at all. We shall never lack good advice so long as we present ourselves week by week before the pulpit. But, in some quarters, we may suffer from the total absence of regular theological instruction in the Faith we profess.

Every educationalist knows that if you do not discipline children in the use of their mother tongue, they will corrupt it with all kinds of slovenliness and incorrectness. That is the drag of Nature. In the same way, if Christians are not disciplined intellectually in the rigorous doctrines of the Church, their interpretations of the Faith will be corrupted by current trends of thought which are both false and undigested. That too is the drag of Nature. The Christian Message is itself corrupted by the philosophical heresies of our time.

Let us see this corruption at work. Consider first that attitude to physical prosperity as the *summum bonum*, which we somewhat loosely call materialism. The world is materialistically-minded. It measures by profit and loss. It believes in measurement by results. When the world tries to create an ethic which is in keeping with its own materialistic evaluations, it naturally creates an ethic based on the antithesis between worldly prosperity and worldly adversity. For instance, in the eighteenth century this worldly ethic became notably popular in our literature. (And of course it has always exercised an influence upon imaginative writers.) Thus novels and plays were written to exemplify the theory that virtue leads to prosperity whilst vice leads to poverty and adversity. This theory encourages a dangerous habit of measuring by results, a habit which is ultimately grounded in materialism and not in the Christian Faith.

Eighteenth-century literature contains some remarkable examples of this ethic. Defoe, professing himself a moralist, wrote novels intended to illustrate how lust and crime lead to poverty and unhappiness. His heroines, Moll Flanders and Roxana, proceed through vicious and sensational careers to experiences of misery and destitution. Thus sin is represented as being unpleasant, not in itself, but in its results. Certain curious implications may follow from the enforcement of this ethic in imaginative literature. We see sin indulged in; and we see misery follow. But how *necessary* is the connection between the sin and the subsequent misery? In Defoe's case it is not necessary at all. We see the excitements of lust and theft, and the consolations which they undoubtedly bring, later "paid for" by imprisonment; but, in point of fact, the imprisonment is really the result of being found out. If the sins had been committed with more circumspection and slightly more luck, then the unfortunate consequences would have been avoided. The appropriate moral lesson which emerges is: If you wish to enjoy the fruits and not the penalties of sin, you must learn to sin efficiently and cunningly.

Even if a direct causal connection is established between sin and subsequent suffering, the moral pattern of a piece of literature cannot be regarded as sound, so long as this subsequent suffering is treated as the main basis for judgement upon the sin. It is true that debauchery may lead to disease and an early death: but ministering to lepers may lead to the same end. It is true that dishonesty can lead to imprisonment and unhappiness: but, with "better luck", it can also lead to wealth and comfort. To discourage sin on the grounds that it is not worth-while in terms of earthly comfort and prosperity is to argue on a false and materialistic basis. Yet this is the implicit ethic of a piece of literature, when the emphasis is put, not upon the evil of sin itself, but upon the unpleasantness to which it can lead. At the worst, in such literature, sin leads to death; and death, by implication, is the worst evil.

Now in thoroughly Christian writers, such as Shakespeare, the crucial sins represented are always intrinsically evil: in Shakespeare's case the poetic overtones emphasize that. Othello's jealousy is plainly evil and unpleasant even before he strangles Desdemona. Macbeth's assassination of Duncan and Leontes' jealousy of Polixenes—these are not enjoyable episodes which happen to bring unpleasant consequences; they are wholly bad in themselves. Moreover, the retribution which follows sin in Shakespeare (in *King Lear* and *A Winter's Tale*, for example) is far from being the thing which makes the whole venture into evil just not worth-while. On the contrary, this retribution for evil often proves to be fruitful of good. From the desolation of suffering springs a burning, purging power. From and through his agony man gains self-knowledge; and true love, loyalty, and unselfishness are recognized for what they are (as they never would have been, without the suffering). Good is born of evil. Pain is revealed as a purging power, and is the background against which true virtue stands most clearly revealed. And death itself is not the greatest evil. Indeed it tends to come as a blessed release from a world where vice—far from leading to adversity and misery—tends to be in the ascendant.

The two ethics are poles apart. In the Christian ethic an evil act is evil *per se*. In the materialistic ethic an act is evil because it brings temporal discomfiture and perhaps even an end to temporal existence. The suffering consequent upon an act, which in the materialistic ethic is itself the evil of the act, proves in the Christian ethic to be potentially good, in that it may restore the sinner through repentance to self-knowledge. Moreover, death, if it follows, proves often to be good in the Christian ethic, in that it comes to one (like Lear) whose spiritual pilgrimage is complete, and who is ready now to leave the place of testing. The trial is over.

This is a very different scheme of thought from that which posits suffering and death as utterly evil—and urges that sin be avoided because it leads to them.

We cannot distinguish good from evil by calculations based on temporal prosperity and adversity. An evil act is evil without reference to the natural or legal penalties it may invoke. It is evil by reference to standards which have the sanction of the supernatural. But unless we consciously keep our morality rooted in the supernatural, it is bound to be corrupted. For otherwise it will root itself in the natural, and we shall measure by material profit and loss, which is the only measurement that unredeemed Nature knows.

Yet who can say that even the life and thought of the Church, the very society of the supernatural, are not constantly corrupted by evaluations at the purely natural level? Have we not come to appraise our acts of public worship for the satisfactions which they give to our emotions and our aesthetic sensibilities? Do we not tend to convert prayer into a mere sequence of petitions and intercessions, so that its value can be measured by the increase in temporal prosperity and comfort to which it appears to contribute? Have we not sympathized with the sophist when he says, "I can see the point of abstaining from beer in Lent, if you give the money saved to some charitable purpose; but there is no advantage [sic] for anyone in your getting up an hour earlier than is necessary"? Are we not prone to excuse even our own minute fulfilments of obligation by a purely natural motive —to claim that even getting up earlier in the morning can be justified on the grounds that it will be conducive to better physical health?

All this results from the intolerable and untiring drag of Nature. A materialistic ethic is an ethic confined by the limits of the natural. Since it has no transcendent values to attach itself to, it focuses the maximum of significance upon temporal prosperity and temporal adversity. There is no escape from an ethic grounded in worldly well-being except by means of an ethic which reaches out to the supernatural.

A false ethic may attempt to disguise its materialistic criteria and naturalistic affiliations: it usually does. The favourite disguise takes the form of an ideal which, though rooted in Nature, masquerades as a mental reality superior to life at the physical level. Thus the psychologists speak of the well-organized or completely integrated personality, and posit ideals of behaviour to which such personalities will conform. It is tempting to believe that the concept of the harmonious personality fulfilled in fruitful activity gives us an ideal superior to the temporal and the physical. But the theorizing of the psychologists, if pressed to its logical conclusion, invariably proves that such is not the case. Their ideal turns out to be a glorification of the natural and the physical. Thus the concept of the harmonious personality compels us to ask with what the personality is in harmony. We shall be told that it is in harmony with its environment. But this is a deterministic and naturalistic ideal. We demand the right to judge our environment. By what standards does the personality which is wholly in harmony with its environment judge that environment? Plainly the concept of a self in harmony with its environment is not an ideal at all. If the environment is bad, the good personality will surely be at war with it. Some of the greatest saints, martyrs, and heroes of history were utterly at loggerheads with their environments. We can scarcely claim that Christ himself achieved that specious kind of "mental health" which is characterized by a harmonious relationship between the self and its environment. We should not praise a man brought up among thieves and racketeers for being in harmony with his environment. And we spend a good deal of breath to-day in blaming the Russian citizen for adapting himself to his environment.

Then too the concept of the personality fulfilled in fruitful activity is equally inadequate. For whom is the activity fruitful? If the activity is fruitful for the self alone, the concept is a perverted one. For some of the worst tyrants, exploiters, and gangsters of history have fulfilled their personalities in activity extremely fruitful for themselves. On the other hand, if the activity is to be fruitful for others, how do we measure what is good for others? Activity which is fruitful for others in a purely worldly sense, increasing their health, prosperity, and comfort, may leave them intellectually barbarous and spiritually moribund. If the fruitfulness of the fulfilled personality's activity is to be measured by the fruitfulness of activity which it encourages in others, then what is the end of all this fruitfulness? A mere stockpiling of undefined fruit is a poor aim for personal activity.

The familiar jargon of the physicians devoted to the cultivation of mental health is all equally reducible to meaninglessness. The concept of the well-organized and completely integrated personality cannot provide a logical ideal. For one thing, the imagery is static: it usually has reference to aesthetic thinking. We think of a great work of art—a great picture, statue, or symphony—as being well organized and integrated. Now the whole point about the picture or the symphony is that it is finished, and that it cannot be altered in any of its parts without detriment. The riches of personality cannot be measured by an ideal so static, passive, and unproductive. If we reject the aesthetic reference of the words, the only other kind of organization and integration left to us is that exemplified in the complex mechanical functioning of the great factory or machine. Here the organization and integration result in fruitful activity; but they are determined in a given pattern, and any slight deviation from the determined pattern would wreck the organization. There is no room for creativity or free will.

The truth is that all these terms in which we describe "mental health" are relative. *Harmonious, integrated, fulfilled, organized, fruitful*—these terms are all inadequate in themselves. They demand some objective point of repose. The self must be in harmony with something, organized and integrated to some end, fulfilled to some purpose, and fruitful of some definite fruit. The self, in short, must be good in relation to some overriding purpose which is to be served by man during his life on this earth. And this purpose will either reckon with man as an inheritor of the Kingdom of Heaven, or ignore his eternal destiny. If this purpose takes no account of man's supernatural vocation, then it can only provide standards of judgement upon human action and human character which are ultimately materialistic. The good (harmonious, integrated, fulfilled, etc.) personality is good because it brings good to others or to itself. Strictly within the limits of the natural, this good can be defined only in terms of material prosperity and physical well-being.

Of course, a worldly ethic is not necessarily either a selfish or a licentious one. Although frankly materialistic, it may lay its emphasis upon the prosperity and well-being of others. In this case, it will obviously produce restrictions upon individual conduct, involving self-control and self-denial. If the individual accumulates too much money, others will have too little: if the individual eats too much, others will starve: if the individual exploits his fellow men, his fellow men are uncomfortable. But the fact that a materialistic ethic imposes restrictions must not blind us to its naturalistic roots. For indeed, even if the emphasis of a naturalistic ethic is upon the prosperity and well-being of the self, without regard to others, there will still be restrictions. If the individual drinks or eats too much, he will make himself ill and shorten his life: if he accumulates too much money, he will burden himself with many cares. A restrictive ethic is not *ipso facto* an exalted altruistic one: still less is it *ipso facto* a supernatural one.

If we press far enough the relative jargon of the mental health physicians, we shall in fact arrive at these ultimates as the root ideal—physical health, comfort, and material prosperity. All the talk about integration, inner harmony, fulfilment, and fruitful activity turns out to be an elaborate disguise for a naturalistic ethic devoted to physical health, comfort, and prosperity. What else can we expect? If our end is not to be eternal well-being, it can only be temporal well-being. The extraordinary thing about the Christian ethic is its utter evasion of deception and disguise. It points straightaway to the supernatural as the only objective point of repose. To do good is to do the Will of God; to do evil is to act against the Will of God. The naked clarity and fundamental simplicity of this principle must not blind us to its comprehensiveness and profundity. Nor, because it imposes restrictions which are uncommonly like the restrictions imposed by a naturalistic ethic, must we make the mistake of confusing the two. To introduce the supernatural as an afterthought, in order to buttress a naturalistic ethic at the point where its foundations begin to be revealed as shaky or non-existent, is a grievous error. Nevertheless it is an error which Christians have grown accustomed to.

That materialistic standards express an ethic which is rooted in the natural, as opposed to the supernatural, is perhaps obvious enough. What is less apparent is that the philosophy of individualism is equally rooted in the natural. Now there is no doubt that the language of popular thinking in psychology, sociology, politics, education, and even religion points to the value of individuality as an ultimate ideal. The significance of the individual, as an isolated source of creative, purposeful activity and of original thought is stressed everywhere nowadays. It is therefore important to

examine the concept of individuality and to see how far it is
founded in a naturalistic philosophy and in what way related
to a philosophy of the supernatural.

In fact, it is not difficult to prove that the popular concept
of individuality is a naturalistic one. As a creature of sense—
as an animal—man is an individual. At the level at which he
eats, drinks, and receives sense-impressions, he is an
individual. But at the level at which he interprets his sense-
impressions in conscious thought he transcends his individualness. For meaning, as we have seen, is a shared
inheritance of the communal consciousness. The meaning
enshrined in language is a communal tradition. Rational
convictions are themselves the inheritance of a social tradition. This tradition is a communal inheritance of values and
standards. In the act of assimilating any part of it, the
individual may be said to enrich his selfhood—but he
enriches his selfhood in the only way in which selfhood can
be enriched, by weakening the isolation and individualness
of the self. One cannot claim any part of a shared inheritance
for one's own without having something more in common
with others. It follows that rational conviction transcends
individual selfhood in such a way that to utter it cannot be
called either self-expression or self-revelation. It would
perhaps be more proper to call it self-annihilation.

This is a crucial point. It is at the sub-rational or animal
level that man is an isolated centre of experience—the
unique focus of sensuous contacts with the natural order and
with his own kind. At the human level—the level of significant consciousness and reflective thought—man enters upon
a shared legacy of meaning and rationality which lifts him
from his isolation. The prime medium of this legacy is
language, and, unless we hold the discredited materialistic
theory of language as a system of labels, we recognize that
all meaning is a communal tradition, which at once sustains

individual consciousness and is enriched by it. It would seem true that, in so far as man is really human, indulging the truly human prerogatives of conscious thought and rational judgement, he is the less isolated in his selfhood. That this is true of man as a moral and spiritual creature has long been known in Christendom. That it is equally true of man as a thinking creature is a corollary which we have long been unwilling to face; but the Christian at any rate ought to be glad that it is so.

There is a strange paradox hidden in this truth, which ought not to be ignored. It is the paradox of freedom. We have long been in the habit of allowing the significance of freedom to be exhausted in the picture of isolated individuals acting independently of one another in accordance with impulses which come from within the individual self. But the thoroughly individual self, as we have seen, is the purely animal centre of sensuous contacts with the physical environment. Thus the individual, *qua* individual, can never know freedom at all. He is wholly determined by those environmental influences so ably investigated by modern psychologists. Man is free only by virtue of exercising choice on the basis of judgement and will. But the standards and values, in accordance with which free choice is made, can be known only through the inheritance of that shared consciousness which links man to his fellows in a community of the centuries. In assimilating the endowment of virtue and rationality which this communal tradition offers, man transcends his individual selfhood. In short, there is no freedom in individualness.

In individualness there is neither freedom nor rationality, neither humanity nor virtue. A philosophy of individualness is a naturalistic philosophy, for it is grounded in the cultivation of man the animal, unexalted above the life of the senses. All significances of the rational and the moral order are attained to by the individual through entry into the communal consciousness, where dwells the shared inheritance of values and meaning.

What, then, are we to make of the individualistic emphases which corrupt so much of contemporary thinking? What but that they manifest the drag of Nature once more. If the philosophy of individualism is utterly naturalistic and hostile to the reality of the supernatural, then indeed we are in an alien world. For our mental climate is alive with assumptions which presuppose a value in the expressiveness and free-play—mental, emotional, and physical—of the individual as an isolated unit of assertiveness.

Thus our political thinking is contaminated by the concept of the autonomous individual, to whose individualness attaches a much-advertised freedom. But, as we have seen, there can be no freedom in pure individualness: man, *qua* individual, is determined: he is free only in so far as he transcends individuality, partaking of that communal inheritance of meaning and value by which free choices can be made. A better word for what the politicians and journalists call "freedom" would perhaps be "independence". For the political individual is conceived as a creature independent of tradition. He can choose whether or not to accept the ethical and spiritual values preserved by his society's traditions, and the obligations and imperatives which they impose. Ironically enough, the individual is considered to reveal his independence most surely in the rejection of these obligations and imperatives. This is a nonsensical view. The tradition, alive in the communal consciousness, which enshrines the cherished values of our culture, is the tradition in whose acceptance we attain to rationality—and therefore to humanity. We may, of course, argue that these values are being betrayed by contemporary perversions of right thinking and right acting. But this is not independence of tradition: it is merely a superior and profounder dependence upon traditional values than our contemporaries seem to accept. Thus all revolution is reaction—except the revolution against meaning and rationality themselves. If I claim that the political system of my society is neither so good nor so just as it ought to be, and work for its reformation, then I am rigorously upholding the significance of *goodness* and *justice* as handed down to me by the communal tradition. I am claiming that these traditional values are being betrayed. Everything therefore which gives weight and significance to my revolutionary activity is derived—not from my individualness or independence—but from my more acute dependence upon a shared tradition.

Perhaps now we can see the popular connotation of the word *independence* disintegrating before our eyes. Independence of a given convention is only the product of a profound dependence upon some more significant tradition. Ultimately, if it is healthy, it is the product of a sensitive dependence upon the significance and reality of certain values —goodness, justice, and truth. Is there any escape from this dependence? There is only one escape from dependence upon the inheritance of values and rationality which are the prerogatives of humanity—and that is the escape to dependence upon the subhuman compulsions of sense, appetite, and possession. This is what we should expect. At the animal level man is an individual. At the animal level man is independent of meaning, reason, and value: he is dependent instead upon physical compulsions.

The political concept of the individual's freedom and independence is thus in itself meaningless. It becomes significant only when it takes cognizance of man's vocation to live by the light of certain values and obligations preserved in the tradition of rationality. That this tradition is rooted in the supernatural is the belief of Christians. It expresses an impulse towards transcendence which the natural order could not of itself produce. For this impulse towards transcendence comes with a judgement upon natural appetite. Moreover, it comes with a judgement upon individualness. And there is no theory in existence—and no theory logically possible—which can explain how evolution could lead natural man, locked in the determined individualness of sensation and appetite, to the invention of significances, values, and obligations which transcend all that he by biological history is.

The question will naturally be asked: Is it not a little out-of-date to attack the political concept of sacred individuality in an age dominated by theories of political collectivism? Without wishing to depreciate the very rich inspiration of Christian charity and fellowship contributing to the social revolution of our time, one must make clear that much socialistic thinking is a mere extension and rationalization of materialistic individualism. In so far as socialistic theory concentrates, not upon man's responsibilities to his fellows, but upon man's individual rights, it is deep dyed in naturalism. Thus much socialistic planning is an elaborate insurance against material discomfort and risk for the individual. The materialistic concept of the socialist State is essentially that of a league of isolated individuals, mutually guaranteeing the inviolability of their individual isolation in satisfaction of sense and appetite. This is a vastly different concept from that of the responsible community of persons united in charity towards the least fortunate members of their society. It is, of course, only fair to point out that, in European countries, the socialist parties combine, often uncomfortably, materialistic individualists and altruistic idealists. The strange admixture of materialism and genuine humanitarianism in the socialist parties of our day makes it particularly difficult for the Christian to place his allegiance conscientiously in contemporary political life. This difficulty is reflected wherever Churchmen enter the political arena, whether as participants or observers.

It has been said that English socialism has roots in nonconformity. Illumination can be drawn from this comment. For, it if may be spoken charitably, the socialist movement seems to reflect the peculiar qualities and the peculiar defects of the dissenting religious bodies. The qualities can be summed up as a righteous indignation against oppression, exploitation, cruelty, and injustice, and a charitable zeal to see the social order manifesting those virtues of brotherly love and fellowship which Christians cherish. It has been the glory of English Dissent that it has refused to allow the creativity of the spirit to be dammed up by convention. The defect of Dissent, from the Anglican point of view, is the weakening of the traditional doctrine of the Church, whose hierarchy, creeds, and sacramental life have always borne witness to its existence as a Divine Society. The weakening of the idea of the Divine Society of persons rooted in the supernatural has indirectly given encouragement to the hope of building a purely temporal society adjusted to the ethical demands of the Christian Faith. Our argument finds this hope to be based upon a misjudgement. The only Christian society is a society rooted in the supernatural: the Church, in fact. The attempt to create a "Christian" society without these roots is self-contradictory. The drag of Nature is too strong. When they are divested of their supernatural affiliation, ideas of the Rights of Man, fair shares for all, and insured socialized welfare inevitably express a naturalistic philosophy, which bespeaks a civilization ignorant of man's supernatural roots.

It is not only in political and sociological thinking that individualistic ideas serve as a cloak for naturalistic heresies. In aesthetic, historical, and educational thinking the same delusive concept flourishes—the concept of the individual as an isolated source of creativity. We are familiar with the cult of so-called "originality" in the literature of aesthetics. The concept of the artistic genius, as it nowadays dominates aesthetic thinking, posits the individual as an ultimate source of creativity, and the value of a work of art is measured by the extent to which it manifests the utter *originality* and *independence* of the creative impulse behind it. A little study of the vocabulary and presuppositions of current aesthetic criticism will reveal that a naturalistic philosophy is not very far in the background. For the creative impulse itself is regularly traced back to the individual's primal experience of the natural order through sensation and appetite. In fact the independence of the artist turns out again to be a dependence upon animal experience of a sub-rational order. In the works of D. H. Lawrence, for instance, there is no attempt to disguise the fundamental dependence of art upon unredeemed sense-experience. But then, as we have seen, if art is to express individualness, it must *ipso facto* be rooted in man's animal life. Only as the artist transcends his individuality can his work manifest the rich significances which reside in the traditions of the communal consciousness. Of course, it is the artist's peculiar duty to enrich the communal tradition with new significances. But these new significances cannot be said to derive from the artist's individuality, which is a centre of uninterpreted sense-experience. Such new significances are created at the conscious level by the illumination of a rare insight: the *giveness* of this insight is itself proof of man's link with the supernatural. This is clearly implicit in the traditional doctrine of an inspiration which comes from above.

The cult of the individual genius is a dangerously misleading one now that it has been separated from any clear sense of the giveness of inspiration. Unless the inspiration is seen as given from above, as a grace redemptive of sense-experience, then it will be regarded as a truly natural growth rooted in individualness. It is important that Christians should do their utmost to cleanse the terminology of aesthetic theory from naturalistic undertones. All theories and interpretations of artistic achievement which make much of imagination, originality, and creativity will point either to the supernatural or to the natural as the source of value and significance. Cleansed of their pseudo-mystical nebulosities and stripped of their rhetorical vagueness, the bulk of current statements about art posit the world of unredeemed Nature as the realm from which life's highest meanings are derived.

The historian is guilty of a similar bias when he treats the human story as primarily a record of progressive assaults upon tradition and convention, by great men from whose isolated individualities sprang a purging and redeeming power. In the individual, as such, there is no source of creative or redemptive power. We have seen that idealistic revolutionary theory and activity are themselves derivative from tradition. The whig-protestant interpretation of history as a progressive debunking and dethroning of dead tyrannies and dead formulas all too often posits the individual rebel and reformer as an isolated source of originality and creativity. Once more we must choose between a natural and a supernatural impulse at the heart of the redemptive act. We cannot exclude Divine Providence from history without introducing the natural order as a source of significances which transcend temporal experience. Yet all that the natural order can convey to man in his pure individualness is the stimulus to sense and the satisfaction of appetite. Significances which transcend, not only the record of sensation, but also the logic of intellectual convention, can come only from above.

The comparable bias of educational theorists towards naturalism has been several times under fire of late. I have investigated the Christian position in this realm in *Repair the Ruins*. There can be no doubt that much unhealthy educational thinking again posits the individual, rooted in sense-experience and locked in the chain of his own biological history, as a source of creativity and value. Talk about "child-centred" education is allowable only if it conceives of the child as a person, inheriting a vocation from the supernatural. Unfortunately it frequently considers the child as an individual growth upon an evolutionary tree. The doctrine of self-expression and "self-motivated" activity [*sic*] is preached on the assumption that within the child's biological individualness resides a secret spring of redemptive meaning and value. The fact that meaning and value are wholly attained through tradition is rarely faced by contemporary educationalists. Still less do they face the fact that their theories of sacred individuality tie the child to the plane of subhuman experience from which it is the business of education to raise him. In short, if current educational theory were fully accepted, with all its ill-digested implications, and if a practice were developed fully consonant with this theory, then education would die out within a few decades. But education survives in defiance of educationalists. The Divine Providence is such that educational theorists are still not taken seriously by the majority of practitioners. There are some teachers who recognize that there is a tradition which transcends individuality, the tradition of value and rationality. In recognizing this, whether they know it or not, teachers are refusing to tie education to a naturalistic philosophy. They testify, by their wise work, to the supernatural affiliations which make a child a person.

As a last example of individualistic heresy, we may quote the popular conception of sexual love. C. S. Lewis has pointed out, in *The Allegory of Love*, that St Thomas Aquinas, like other medieval scholars, found a theological difficulty impeding attempts to treat sexual love as being of sacramental significance. The difficulty, for them, lay in the fact that there is an irrational element in sexual love. Sexual intercourse is an experience in which man's animal sensuality seems to govern him so completely that the rule of reason is temporarily in abeyance. What is especially interesting, as Lewis points out, is that the very thing which for the moderns sanctifies love—its capacity to dominate the whole man in an irrational and ungovernable passion—is precisely the thing which made sexual love suspect to the medieval theologian. It is not our business here to try to clear up this particular theological difficulty. That an orthodox theology of romantic love can be propounded has been proven in the work of Charles Williams. Our concern is with the fact that a passion grounded in individual sensuality is popularly invested with a transcendental religious significance by naturalists who would be unwilling to accord a supernatural significance to anything else in human experience.

The very writers and thinkers who ground sexual love most surely in man's animal experience at the natural level tend to give this love a sanction which transcends values and obligations of a rational kind. This love, rooted in animal sensuality, is granted a value to which the ties of filial duty, the marriage bond, and responsibility for positive temporal achievement are rendered subordinate. In short, a sanction is given to a purely natural passion which Nature herself cannot logically provide. This sanction is paraded by the popular novelists, high-brow, middle-brow, and low-brow alike. It may come protected by a frank philosophy of man's animality as his highest endowment, as it does in D. H. Lawrence. Or it may come sheltered and concealed by a perverse vocabulary of pseudo-mystical, pseudo-metaphysical nebulosities, as it does in Charles Morgan. In either case the Christian must recognize a naturalistic philosophy no more exalted, and little more coherent, than that which underlies the vapid sentimentalities of the daily press.

The all-pervasive infection of individualism in the popular climate of opinion could itself form the subject of a substantial volume. We have traced this infection far enough to realize what a damaging influence it represents. It attempts to ground value in the individual self as a focus of sense-impressions, whence no value can derive. Value, we believe, is grounded in the objective order, not as given to the individual in sensation, but as interpreted by the communal consciousness in the light of its own traditions of meaning and rationality. Value, in fact, represents the impingement of the supernatural upon the natural order. Its existence testifies to the Divine Creation of man's world. In order to attain to realization of value, man transcends his individuality and interprets his experience in the light of a common tradition of meaning and rationality. The existence of this meaning and rationality within the comprehension of the human mind testifies to the Divine Creation of man himself. Man, as rational, is rooted in the supernatural as surely as spiritual man.

Thus we recognize individualism and materialism as peculiarly the philosophies of the natural and the finite, shut off from grace, transcendence, and redemption. At the animal level of sensation and appetite man is truly an individual; and therefore individualism is the philosophy of naturalism. At this same level, man seeks only to manipulate and loot his world in the interests of sensual satisfaction and individual survival: and therefore materialism is the philosophy of naturalism. As these are peculiarly the philosophies of the natural, so they are the philosophies of the finite. For time splits up the integrated personality into a discrete sequence of individual experiences of the phenomenal world. Man is human only in transcendence of time's limitations. Only through the exercise of memory and foresight is man rational and purposeful. Only through the inheritance of the collective conscious traditions which survive the passing centuries does man attain to knowledge, wisdom, and culture. Nature and finitudes are, in themselves, hostile to the cultivation of man's manhood. And especially are they hostile to man's supernatural affiliations.

A danger of religious thinking is that it may widen the gap between the natural and the supernatural. For if it sees Nature and finitude only in their negative aspects as hostile to Supernature, it can lead only to despair. Christianity recognizes that Nature and finitude have a positive as well as a negative potentiality. Though Nature and finitude are *in themselves* hostile to Supernature, they are capable of redemption and transfiguration. The doctrine of Incarnation preserves the delicate balance of a position midway between that of religions which utterly reject the order of Nature, and that of religions which find salvation in Nature. Naturalism is evil, not because it accords value to the natural, but because it accords such value to the natural *in itself*. Therefore it is true, in a sense, to say that naturalism is evil, not because it points in the wrong direction, but because it does not point far enough. Indeed when the prophet of Nature, moved by the grandeur and beauty of the natural order, points beyond these qualities to some eternal reality which they manifest, then his position is likely to become, in this matter, indistinguishable from the Christian's position. Hence Wordsworth, condemned as a pantheist by some, is acclaimed as a Christian teacher by others.

What is true of the prime heresy of naturalism, is true of the subordinate and derivative heresies of materialism and individualism. Man's animal individuality is evil only if it is cultivated exclusively: it can be redeemed by being taken under the direction of a will orientated to the supernatural.

Again the material order is evil only if it is served exclusively: its attractions can be transfigured by being subsumed into a significant pattern entangled in the supernatural. Naturalism, individualism, and materialism are evil because they are finite philosophies which exclude Supernature. But Nature, the individual man, and the attraction of the material world can each alike be transfigured and redeemed.

We have spoken of the delicate balance which Incarnation represents. It is a balance between forces potentially hostile to each other and yet capable of mutual alliance. This balance can be easily upset. The thesis of this book as a whole is that naturalism is so rife to-day that the Christian Message is often corrupted as a result of the proper attempt to make a helpful ally of a potential foe. In other ages other dangers were more predominant. We can think of historical periods when Christendom was in greater danger of rejecting Nature utterly than of coming too easily to terms with her. Now, however, the situation is different. We do not generally need to exhort ourselves or our brethren to beware of blaspheming God's creation through excessive asceticism and mortification of the flesh. Rather we need to be continually on our guard lest the drag of Nature tug a too pliant Christian dogma from its roots in the supernatural.

Perhaps, as a last illustration of how insidious this drag of Nature can be, we may point to popular current interpretations of the fundamental spiritual virtues, Faith, Hope, and Love. Surely no words point more clearly to the supernatural than do these three, when they are invested with their rightful Christian connotations. Each virtue directs the soul to God. Faith is faith in God, in the transcendent significance of the supernatural. Hope is hope in God, in the ultimate rightness, stability, and security of the supernatural order. Love is love of God and love of other men in God— love of one's fellows by virtue of the common sonship of a heavenly Father. And yet each of these three terms is commonly and frequently degraded by the drag of Nature, so that even Christian controversy and Christian preaching are not free of the taint of naturalism.

Man as an individual, man as a finite creature of Nature, is one who lives by *getting* and flourishes by *having*. Materialistic possessiveness dominates his life in Nature. When *Faith* is disentangled from its supernatural roots and dragged down to the natural level, then it becomes a mere confidence in the security of possessions. "You must have faith", we are told, when we are wondering whether our finances will hold out or our shares will keep their level, when we are trembling on the brink of ill-health or physical discomfiture. It is true that we must have faith, in situations of world adversity. But faith is not just an irrational confidence in future temporal well-being. Nor is faith even merely individual confidence in eternal felicity as a future possession. When the concept of Faith is exploited at the level at which we *get* and *have*, it is inevitably perverted. Any element of possessiveness is hostile to true faith, which is the virtue by which man makes a supreme and utter self-committal to the supernatural.

Again, when *Hope* is dragged down to the natural level, at which man is hag-ridden by the urge to possess, it becomes an empty label for giving a mystical sanction to selfish desire. It becomes an irrational confidence in the future temporal security of the *having* ego. Gabriel Marcel has made a most illuminating study of the second Christian Virtue in *Homo Viator*. Under the title *A Metaphysic of Hope* he analyses the insidious tendency to divest Hope of its supernatural orientation by making it subservient to the individual and the material. We must neither *hope that* nor *hope for*. As Christians, we must merely hope—in God, of course. Hope is a selfless trust, undefined by possessive impulse,

132

disentangled from egoistical desire. It is grounded in penitence and wholly directed to God.

Finally, the Christian Virtue of *Love* is particularly debased in common thinking to-day. When the concept of Love succumbs to the drag of Nature, God is left out of the picture. Love is rationalized by the possessive individual into the wilful impulse that demands fair shares for all, as the likeliest way of ensuring individual inviolability. The general temporal security of others is seen as an indirect safeguard of the possessive ego's well-being. Love is thus entangled in Nature by man's worldly possessiveness. Yet in reality Love is the virtue of self-giving in all situations, a virtue marked by selfless committal to the supernatural. This committal involves a trust which shatters the dominion of possessiveness. Consider the lilies of the field.

If one thing emerges from this survey, it is that, in the present climate of opinion, Christians need to be continually, alertly and (if the word may be redeemed) aggressively conscious that their religion is a religion of the supernatural. It is not a religion with a mere supernatural background; not a religion with a mere supernatural promise: it is a religion entangled in the supernatural from its roots up. The time has gone by when this fact could be taken for granted in controversy between Christians and non-Christians. It is a frightening and intolerable thing to say; but there are signs that the time has also gone by when this fact could be taken for granted among Christians themselves—if the name is allowed to all who claim it. Let us recognize the situation in which we live. When we press the claims and reality of the supernatural, our non-Christian acquaintances will regard us as the victims of irrational superstitition. Any kind of testimony to the supernatural is an admission of superstition in the eyes of most of our contemporaries. That is the reason why the modernist "concessions" no longer cut any ice. The contemporary materialist is not impressed by the fine distinctions which allow Christ's Divinity and question his capacity to act divinely.

We must be prepared, then, to be labelled superstitious by non-Christians. No midway drawing of the line—between one claim to the miraculous and another—can make the Christian Faith respectable now among thorough-going materialists. But this is perhaps the least uncomfortable fact of our present situation. For, if we press the overriding reality of the supernatural, many of our fellow-Christians will regard us as guilty, not perhaps of superstition, but of a kind of lack of reticence akin to indecency. What is true may still, if spoken about openly, be condemned as indelicate. There are things which one does not discuss in respectable company. One cannot but sense that the utter entanglement of Christianity in the supernatural has become one of those uncomfortable truths which many Christians feel it improper to utter publicly. There are people who can bear to be thought superstitious, but who have an understandable horror of being judged indelicate. Many age-old restraints are now called unhealthy inhibitions, which Christians are proud to cherish. But there is here an inhibition which they can join with the psychologists to throw off.

The mysteries of omnipotence and freedom stretch the human reason to the limits of its grasp. We do not know how far Providence can be said to be "limited" by the failure of free human beings to offer their willing co-operation. We can never tell how often the Divine impulse of Grace fails to reach man because there is no human prayer to open the way. Still less can we guess in what manner and in what measure the open transfiguration of the finite order by the supernatural is held off by the blindness of man to the super-natural reality. If the impingement of Supernature upon Nature seems to be little in evidence to our waking eyes, is this not itself a sign of the weakness of our faith? The Christian answer to the greatest question of our time is really a very simple one. The lack of overt evidence of the supernatural and the lack of faith in the supernatural are not two isolated facts with a causal connection. They are two complementary aspects of man's failure to resist the drag of Nature.

5

THE CHURCH

IN ENGLAND to-day there is an astonishing ignorance of what the Church really is. If Churchmen wish to see what the Church looks like to the masses outside, they must first dismiss from their minds everything that is really significant about their membership of a Christian Body. They must forget about Baptism, Regeneration, the sacraments, and self-dedication in a Divine Society, to which they belong as surely as do bishops and priests. They must see the Church as a network of buildings, staffed by a body of professional clergymen. They must see these buildings visited weekly by a small percentage of the population. Visited for what purpose? Here ideas are generally vague. That some people like to sing hymns—this will be patronizingly granted by the majority: that some people seriously look to a blessed future state which is somehow tied up with Church attendance during man's earthly pilgrimage—this will be grudgingly conceded by a large number: that some people believe themselves better than their neighbours because they attend Church regularly—this will be ironically acclaimed by a noisy minority. But that there are people who seriously believe that in the life of the Church they root their own existences out of Nature and out of time—this idea is utterly foreign to the nation as a whole.

It is a pity. For if the real claims of the Church as a Divine Society were more widely understood, there would surely be less apathy before the religious issue. If the stupendous claim of Churchmen to root their daily lives in an order beyond the finite were noised abroad, it would arouse hostility, scorn, bewilderment, and ridicule; but it would surely discourage apathy. Indeed it would provoke, as well as hostility, an uneasy self-questioning likely to be fruitful in conversions.

In considering what the Church looks like to our contemporaries, we must again take into account the peculiar characteristics of the civilization in which we live. The developments of the last hundred years have changed the face of England. A century ago there were comparatively few institutions of any kind which spread a network over the country as a whole. There were fewer opportunities therefore for the growth of misleading conceptions of the Church as a national institution. Nowadays, to the undiscerning, the Church is one among an increasing number of "institutions" with "branches" in every corner of the kingdom. We may mention the Post Office, the Labour Exchanges, the Food Offices, and the Registry Offices. Banks, Building Societies, and Insurance Companies have similar networks. And, though they are less frequently represented by buildings, political parties and trade unions are finely and efficiently organized on a national scale.

It is in the company of national organizations such as these that the Church presents itself to many of our contemporaries. You get your Family Allowance at the Post Office, you get your car licensed at the Motor Taxation Department, and you get married in Church. That is one aspect of the Church alive in the popular mind. It exists to provide what have, oddly enough, come to be known as "public services". It dispenses christenings and marriages as other institutions dispense concentrated orange juice or vacancies for employment. Another living aspect of the

Church is that it makes a call for support, rather as the political parties and the trade unions do, and as the hospitals used to do. The difference is that the Church seems to offer so little in return for this support. The hard-headed citizen can see what he gets from his trade union; he recognizes the need for hospitals; he is prepared to put his hand in his pocket for cripples, orphans, and the blind. But can the Church be said to use its resources chiefly for alleviating poverty and caring for the sick? And, in any case, has not social insurance generally obviated the need for indiscriminate almsgiving?

There is no need to reproduce at length the crudest popular misconceptions of what the Church is. They all amount to the same thing. The Church is viewed as a purely human institution with a double function——that of providing certain unnecessary but pleasing ceremonies to mark the turning-points in domestic and national life; and that of serving certain humanitarian ends in relation to the sick and needy at home and abroad.

Unfortunately misconceptions about the meaning of the Church are not confined to the uneducated. They are largely shared by the educated too. Error is so widespread that continual emphasis is needed upon the fact that the Church is a Divine Society pre-eminently concerned with worship and prayer, with the preservation and nourishment of the spiritual life, with the revelation of Incarnation, Redemption, and Salvation. No good can come of belittling the Church's claim or of toning down her supernatural purpose. If the Church is to evangelize this kingdom, she must learn again to shock, to stun, to stupefy by the enormity and audacity of her claims. If she is not, root and branch, devoted to a supernatural end, then she is devoted to natural ends; she is just another organization for the amelioration of social and material conditions.

Churchmen must, above all, learn not to defend the Church for the wrong reasons. "The Church has not achieved for the working man social reforms comparable to those achieved by the Labour Party." The proper reply is, "Of course not". "The Church is not devoting all its energies to the prevention of war, to the conquest of cancer, to the abolition of the death-penalty." The proper reply is, "Of course not". "The clergy do not spend half their time in social and humanitarian work." Again, the proper reply is, "Of course not".

The Church must be defended in controversy for her continual and proper preoccupation with her own business. Her clergy must be defended for their daily persistence in worship and prayer, how ever little observed by others. They must be defended for their regular obedience to our Lord's absolute command at the Last Supper. What else is the duty of the Christian Church, if not obedience to such commands? The significance of prayer and sacrifice, vicariously offered even on behalf of railers and scoffers, must be everywhere re-called. The reply may well be—"What does it matter any-way?" If so, well and good: we have at least got to grips with the real problem, with the meaning of the Church. We are no longer at sea in a storm of misconceptions about social reform.

Of course the Church's own record in humanitarian work is magnificent too. The informed Churchman can point to heroism and self-sacrifice in the Church's service to the sick and destitute, which speak of a power more than human. It is well that this record should be spoken of. But behind it lies a reservoir of spiritual power fed by prayer, worship, and dedication to the life of the spirit. And this life is the Church's first concern. On the nourishment of this alone can the Church be judged. And since no human authority can ever measure the things of the spirit, it follows that the Church can never be judged here below.

This needs to be said, for there is the danger that the life of the spirit will be regarded as a means to a purely temporal end—the accomplishment of good works among the sick and needy. It is true that these good works are the fruits of our faith: indeed our faith compels us to undertake them. But, though the Church must never cease to urge us to works of mercy and philanthropy, we on our part must not imagine that she exists simply to initiate and encourage activities whose results can be measured in terms of temporal well-being.

The first significance of the Church is that she perpetuates through history the Divine Incarnation. She offers to twentieth-century man what our Lord offered uniquely to his disciples during his earthly life—the opportunity to live in him. It follows logically and necessarily from this that the life of the Church will be fruitful in good works. Our Lord went about healing all manner of sickness among men, comforting the poor and destitute, and befriending the weak and helpless. A true perpetuation of his Incarnation involves continual occupation with works of mercy. But it is devastatingly illogical and obtuse to make invidious comparisons between the Church's official achievements in medical and social work and those of the great hospitals and homes for the sick and the maimed. Our Lord healed the sick when they were brought to him: but we are not told that he set out on a great Faith-healing tour. He comforted the needy; but he did not give himself to social agitation. He blessed every impulse of charity towards the poor; but he did not organize a system of soaking the rich on their behalf. It may be right for the State to constitute itself an elaborate mechanism for ironing out economic inequalities by all manner of taxation. But our Lord himself, intent upon salvation, never played at Robin Hood. For one thing, we may be sure that he would have considered soaking the rich far too easy on the rich. His word to the rich—and he spoke to none more harshly—was a sterner one. "Sell all thou hast and give to the poor. . . ." "It is easier for a camel to pass through the eye of a needle. . . ." Wilful self-deprivation is the only way.

There is small cause therefore for Churchmen to blush with shame (except on their own personal account) before the popular accusation that the Church has played no part in the great social revolution that has produced the Welfare State. For one thing, the accusation is not true; for wherever individual Churchmen work in the social and political spheres, there one may see the hand of the Church. The clergy would be false to their calling if they concentrated first and foremost on work of this kind. Moreover, it is impossible to measure the fruits of the Church's worship and witness—even the fruits in social amelioration. Who can say what has been the indirect effect of the Church's prayer and praise upon the movements which have made our civilization, corporately and officially, more tender to the sick and maimed, more considerate to the unhinged criminal, more sensitive to the needs of the very young and the very old? Christians must believe that such improvements have matured under God's Providence. What resources of Grace have been released into the body politic by the worship and sacramental life of the Church, by the contemplation, prayer, and self-dedication of her communities—this we can never know, and perhaps we ought not to ask.

For even as we hint at the possible social fruits of the Church's worship and witness, we walk on a razor-edge above the chasm of heresy. We can scarcely touch upon the subject without implying that the Church's life is a means to an earthly end. And in this implication are rooted all contemporary errors about the function and effectiveness of the Church. We have said that contemporary civilization and the climate of thought it has bred work together towards the despiritualization of human endeavour and aspiration. How dangerous to Christian thinking is the prevailing habit of dismissing the supernatural has been made abundantly clear. At all points the drag of Nature corrupts human thinking to the state in which it measures all things by worldly results, orientating even the spiritual virtues of Faith, Hope, and Love towards the realm of material prosperity and adversity. The concept of the Church suffers such a complete adulteration by materialistic and naturalistic thinking that the first significance of the Church, as a society rooted in the supernatural order, is popularly ignored. The world measures by ostensible results, by earthly profit and loss, so that where the Church is not regarded as a great organization devoted to humanitarian ends, it is looked upon as an institution for purveying moral advice, with a view to distributing passports to Heaven.

Though we may regret the limited view of the Church as an agency which qualifies its members for a future life of undefined bliss, it is at least healthier than the view of the Church as an organ of social reform. At least it directs our gaze beyond the finite. But it is grossly inadequate none the less. The vision of a future life as an indefinite continuation of temporal felicity is itself tainted with materialism. Once more it is based upon profit-and-loss calculations, though the profits are posited beyond the grave. The Church comes to be regarded as a vast Correspondence college, which can qualify us externally for graduation in the eternal university. It subjects us, however, to risks which other more commercial agencies of this kind are careful to avoid. For there is no guarantee that our money will be refunded if we fail to pass in the final test.

Among current misconceptions of the Church's significance it would be wrong not to mention the popular view of the Church as an educational institution, devoted to the task of moral exhortation. This view represents the Church as a preaching institution, burdened with the pre-eminent duty to issue moral exhortations in the face of increasing divorce, vice, gambling, and the like. Now this conception of the Church as a tool for moral rearmament is tainted by materialism and by heretical individualism. The corruption of materialism shows itself in the fact that moral rearmament is advertised as a means to an earthly end—as a surer way to the establishment of peace, prosperity, and brotherhood than any programme put forward by the politicians. The corruption of individualism shows itself in the fact that this view assumes in man a capacity for self-perfecting which he does not possess. Moreover it leads in popular preaching to a disastrous tendency to urge Christians to go out and improve their neighbours. Anyone who has been submitted in public worship to sermons and prayers which continually picture the faithful as able to illumine the dark places of God's earth by the force of their moral example, will realize how fraught with dangers this emphasis can be. Prefaced by the call to repentance and surrender to the Will of God, the exhortation to go out and shed the light of goodness upon the children of darkness can perhaps be discreetly made. Divested of its penitential and self-dedicating preliminaries, it is a presumption quite diabolical in magnitude. Such a slight shift of emphasis takes the meat out of Christian teaching. Such a delicate shade of thoughtlessness in the use of words ministers to bad thinking where only good was intended. One hesitates to quote examples from experience. But it is in the particular that these misconceptions do their damage, and clarity has claims as well as charity. One may question therefore whether the right message on the Feast of St Mary Magdalen in a too-comfortable middle-class parish is provided by the prayer that "We too, like Our Lord, may have compassion upon sinners". Are we associates of the forgiving, sinless God; or are we, too, sinners asking for mercy? It is such a little thing, this thoughtless false emphasis, yet time after time it may bring us down firmly on the wrong side of the fence. Or rather it may bring us down on the right side of the fence, when we know in our souls that we belong on the other side.

Here again the traditional doctrines of the Church exist to keep us on the right path. From the doctrine of Grace we learn that man, in his own right, is incapable either of reforming himself or of reforming others. He does not go to Church to learn how to force himself and others into virtue. He goes to Church to repent and to ask for the gift of that life in God by which he may be used in accordance with the Divine Purpose. He goes to root himself in the life of an order beyond the world, to feed on the food of the spirit. The instruction he needs tells of his own unworthiness and the fact of Redemption achieved. He must will to share, not in a grand Crusade to redeem, but in the fruits of an already given Redemption. He must strive to hope—how much against the grain it goes—that he may share infinitesimally in the sacrifice of Love which is mankind's atonement.

Since so much has been said in this book about the dangers of regarding the Church simply as an institution devoted to temporal or humanitarian ends, it is perhaps necessary to point out that it is equally dangerous to picture the Church as a Divine Society, if we are thereby led to despise or neglect works of charity, mercy, and social reform. If a single reader were left with the impression that a Churchman can afford to close his eyes, his hands, or his pockets before the crying evils of poverty, sickness, ignorance, and affliction, then it would be better that this book had not been written. It is almost an illogicality to say that faith without works is useless; for indeed faith without works is not faith at all. Faith is self-committal to the Will of God, and the lives of a thousand saints and a million devout souls bear witness that, once the self-committal is achieved, God will direct the committed believer to all manner of humane services to his fellow men.

If we imagine, as we begin to discipline our souls in membership of the Church, that there is going to be any conflict between the claims of God upon us and the claims of the poor, the underfed, the diseased, or the delinquent, then we are making a very serious mistake: and it will not be long before we realize that it is so. Of course it is theoretically possible to picture a man sitting in his armchair at the fireside, wondering whether to spend the evening worshipping at church or visiting prisoners in the local gaol. Indeed, one might comfortably consume a whole evening revolving this problem, and finally go to bed, having decided that it is too difficult to choose between such desirable alternatives. But it is not the man of faith who spends his time like that. He has other things to do. Those Christians who have worked most heroically for the diseased and the down-trodden will be the first to admit—not that by faith they acquired this practical virtue—but that, having given themselves to God, he used them thus.

"The truth is, that both faith and works are needed; but works are the result of faith, not a substitute for it." Dr Moss sums the issue up in these few words in *The Christian Faith*. By pressing the claims of supernatural religion we are not diverting energy from the field of practical charity. On the contrary, we know that by this means alone can new energies be released into the sphere of humanitarian endeavour. Through self-committal in obedience and worship, Christians will find themselves used for charitable works of undreamed-of scope and intensity. It will be when we come truly to know and experience the Church as the Body of Christ, and ourselves as very members thereof, that the Church will become that effective organ of humanitarian service and ministration which, without that knowledge and experience, we strive in vain to make it.

It is not within the scope of this book to attempt a tidy analysis of the doctrine of the Church; but a survey such as this can end constructively only by turning to the Church, which must be the bulwark against all the evils we have investigated. We have seen the drag of Nature as the dominating evil of our day, embracing all kinds and degrees of materialistic and individualistic heresies. The only resistance to the drag of Nature is the power of Supernature. The danger for us is that, through submission to the naturalistic *Zeitgeist*, we shall forget to mention whence salvation comes. Yet any tendency to disguise or soft-pedal the supernatural reality of the Christian Religion is a corruption so congenial to the twentieth-century mentality that it will spread and increase like a contagion. At the core of resistance to this disease must always stand the Church, as a living Body of men and women who, with all their frailties and stupidities, are in some little measure striving to root their lives in the supernatural.

Any attempt to particularize in detail about the significance of the Church would lead to involvement in inter-denominational and even intra-denominational controversy of a kind which a book like this is probably better without. But it will be clear to all earnest Christians that a Christian Body cannot disentangle itself from the supernatural without ceasing to practise a religion at all. And, in using the word *religion* thus, one stumbles upon a convenient summary of the issue. Because, put quite simply, the problem of England at the present time would seem to lie in the question whether

Christianity is to remain a religion, or is to be diluted and despiritualized into a philosophy and a social programme.

It can do no good to disguise the fact that to many men who claim to be Christians—many wiser and utterly better than we who thus criticize them—Christianity is no longer a *religion* at all. Nowhere perhaps is this clearer than in the educational world, where lip-service is paid to Christianity on an almost unprecedented scale. It is paid by good, hard-working, unselfish, idealistic men who try to do their utmost for those whom they serve and those over whom they exercise authority. Yet their lip-service is in most cases either intellectual approval of a noble humanitarian philosophy or moral zeal for an inspiring and altruistic ethic. By all purely natural criteria it is good, even fruitful. It would be disastrous were we to be deprived of this restraining and stabilizing influence in our civilization. But *it does not represent a religion*, which is, *ipso verbo*, an orientation of personal life to a reality beyond the confines of temporal existence.

Wherever the Church meets culture, wherever the Church meets civilization, to bless its endeavours, to share in some common movement towards the amelioration of man's lot, there will arise the danger that the fundamentally *religious* character of Christianity will be obliterated. Where an established Church plays such a notable part in national life, in relation to the monarchy, the parliament, the law-courts, the armed forces, and the educational system, the danger is especially acute that its *raison d'être*, as the expression of personal and corporate religious life, will be overlooked. In short, the Church is more in danger of being weakened by shallow patronage than of succumbing before deep-seated hostility.

For here the drag of Nature meets us once more, in an even more subtle form. When soul meets body, the spirit may redeem the body or the body may destroy the soul. When the Church is ever at hand to bless the official endeavours of secular civilization, the spiritual Body may redeem civilization, or civilization may desupernaturalize the Church.

The risk must be taken. But it need not be taken blindly. The Church will remain a religious body as long as its members are practising a religion. And we in the Church of England are blessed in the realization that, in the twentieth century, when our Church has been accused of being content to lend an air of vague religiosity to public life, it has been immeasurably enriched by the growth of communities, which guarantee the nourishment and increase of its inner spiritual resources. Indeed the growth of community life in the Church of England must probably be accounted the most significant thing in the religious history of twentieth-century England. This reservoir of spiritual vitality is especially needful to a Church which pays the price of Incarnation so dutifully through the medium of Establishment.

No one can read the theological works of different contemporary denominations without realizing that the mere fact of a divided Church is not a source of spiritual danger comparable to that represented by the ubiquitous desupernaturalizers of the Faith. It is not hard for the Christian to meet in charity and sympathy with those who would lay their emphases differently from his own. Where some stress the significance of the Church's sacraments as channels of Divine Grace, others stress the significance of non-liturgical private meditation. It is possible to believe such differences of emphasis fruitful in the spiritual life of Christendom. But any hint of desupernaturalizing the Christian Message and the Christian Life raises controversy of an utterly different order. There is no question then of studying another community's recommendations about the surest means offered to man for repentance and self-surrender, the surest way to achieve a share in the flood of Divine Grace released by our

Lord's Atonement. When the hand of Nature assails the Christian Church, to disentangle it from its supernatural roots, it is time for resistance, and perhaps for a drastic surgical operation.

There is so much painful history behind religious controversy that we perhaps ought to be glad to see the approach of an issue which will unite Christians across many barriers. If there is no such issue even now upon us, this book is based upon a grave misunderstanding. And the issue, as I see it, is whether Christians who have a supernatural religion are going to be swamped by "Christians" who have only a humanistic philosophy of life. No doubt the issue will before long bring into prominence in the Church of England the doctrine of the Church as the Mystical Body and the question of the Establishment. It will be linked too with controversy about inter-denominational activities and possible reunion with the Free Churches. It will be confused probably by a growing opinion in the popular mind that "Christian" is the proper label for a man who is neither a Communist nor an extreme left-wing Socialist.

Controversy is not to be feared. Confusion, on the other hand, is to be dreaded. And especially the menace of a confusion which blurs the difference between a religion and a philosophy, a religion and a social programme, a religion and a moral code. One is tempted to hope that controversy of a certain kind will increase. Let us have more controversy: but let it be *religious* controversy. We should perhaps be less in danger of losing sight of essentials, if we were hard at each other's brains about Grace and Freewill, the doctrine of the Eucharist, the Apostolic Succession, and the meaning of priestly Absolution.

Those who accuse Churchmen of slavery to superstition, those who criticize the Church for preservation of dogma from the pre-scientific age, those who charge the Church with being intellectually out-of-date and incapable of adjusting itself to the forward movements of modern knowledge— these critics are to be resisted without compromise, for in reality their charges amount to this: that Christianity is too much involved in the supernatural, that the Church is being so wrong-headed as to try to preserve a religion in a scientific age. But there are critics of an utterly different calibre, within the Church and without, who come with charges and warnings which it would be well for us to listen to. These are the critics who accuse the Church of being too much involved in the natural, and who warn us against all those aspects of institutional organization and activity which seem incongruous with the practice of an other-worldly religion.

There are distinguished and honoured names among those who have criticized the Church on these grounds. Kierkegaard has warned us of the danger that a temporal institution, established in history and preserving an historical revelation, may obscure the eternal contemporaneousness of the Christian challenge. According to Kierkegaard, the danger to the Church, as a temporal institution, is not only that she may obscure the true contemporaneousness of God's redeeming work, but also that, by her very institutional and historical existence, she may cease to present the call of a Christ incarnate in humiliation, and may present only the call of a Christ remote in glory.

In a more strictly philosophical vein, Berdyaev argues that the objectivization of the Christian Revelation in an earthly institution opens the door to a perverted, even diabolical idolatry of the finite masquerading as the infinite. Just as aesthetic beauty, erotic love, or human knowledge may be falsely absolutized as the object of adoration which ought properly to reach beyond the finite to the infinite, so the Church herself, as a social institution, may enslave the soul of man to a finite idolatry. In other words, Berdyaev warns us of the paradoxical danger that the menace of perverted materialism threatens even at the heart of obedience to the supernatural authority residing in the Church.

These warnings are not quoted because they represent the present writer's point of view. They are reproduced in the hope of clarifying a line of criticism directed against the Church which it is urgently necessary to distinguish from less positive criticism. We may rest assured that if we ourselves do not distinguish between constructive and destructive criticism of the Church, our modernist enemies will make capital out of our confusion. Writers such as I have quoted, then, are not in the least afraid of what the pseudo-scientific critics consider to be the superstitious and irrational element in the claims of the Christian Church. They are certainly not worried lest the Church involve herself too inextricably by dogma and practice in the demands of an undemonstrable supernatural order. Their fear is the very opposite of this. It is the fear that the Church, as a human institution, may become so subtly and firmly involved in the natural that the other-worldly character of the Christian Faith is weakened and jeopardized. Theirs is not the modernist's dread lest Christianity should again become a religion: theirs is the fear that Christianity may cease to be a religion.

There is another distinction which may conveniently be pointed to in this context. It is the subtle distinction between those who attack the Church's dogmatic clarity and certainty because it exceeds the scope of scientific knowledge, wherein all their faith is reposed, and those who are hesitant and reluctant before dogmatic clarity and certainty because it seems to them to play presumptuously with the incomprehensible mystery of the Godhead and to intellectualize too glibly the profound realities of personal religious experience. The former attack springs from pride and ignorance—a pride which over-estimates the capacity of mankind for putting the whole universe at the service of experiment and manipulation, and an ignorance of the proper limits and applicability of the scientific method. The latter reluctance springs from humility and awe. It is often rooted in spiritual experience of a profound order. The need to make this distinction between two attitudes which have a superficial similarity is of tremendous importance. From one side come charges and misunderstandings which call for the resistance of authority and the voice of instruction. From the other side come warnings which call us—not to resistance and emphatic teaching—but to acute self-questioning and humble prayer.

For here again, in these attacks upon dogmatic clarity and certainty, two utterly different impulses are at work. In the guise of pseudo-scientific modernism, the dark powers of unredeemed Nature have supernatural religion by the throat. Whilst, at the same time, from the hearts and minds of those who are sensitive to the mystery and reality of the supernatural, come timely reminders of the supreme need for humility and awe before the incomprehensible wonder of the Godhead.

The Church, as a Body of men and women living the life of the spirit through worship and sacrament, can never judge what is the effect of its practice and prayer upon contemporary life. But the Church as a teaching institution, presenting in intellectual terms the challenge of the supernatural to a secular civilization, can certainly measure its success in subverting the false philosophies of the day. The fruits of the Church's spiritual life can be seen only by God. But the immediate results of the Church's intellectual appeal can be roughly measured here and now. We have argued that, in this domain, the Church's message must be presented as an uncompromising challenge from the supernatural to all who are earthbound in the false self-sufficiency of the finite. The Church must be prepared to shock people out of this false self-sufficiency, to shift them uneasily from their shallow roots in the finite, to lift them above Nature and to shake them out of time. Whether, in the long run, the Church will be clearly called to cease to bolster secular civilization by her blessings upon civil affairs and her acceptance of official status, cannot be known as yet. But clearly the call is already upon her to oppose the prevailing naturalistic philosophies which, having corrupted our social and intellectual culture, now threaten her own message and her own status as the *Civitas Dei*.

The impact of the "Christian view" of life will never shake our civilization unless it is truly the Christian view— in other words, unless it is the religious view of life. But the power of the true Christian view of life for cleansing our culture is enormous. It is a view full of excitements and adventurous new insights. It is fraught too with unexpected dethronements and unexpected rehabilitations. It carries a whole cargo of Chestertonian paradoxes with which to overturn the capricious idolatries and the facile debunkings of every brand of glib modernism. For the Christian view of life reveals alike that the staunchest conservative is only just beginning to learn what there is to conserve in human tradition, and that the most radical revolutionary is a baby at the game of discovering what there is to uproot and destroy.

For what is the preservation of a constitution or a social culture, to those who are involved in preserving the revelation of the risen Christ, the priesthood, the Word, and the sacrament by which men may yet live in the power of the Resurrection? What is the assault upon Capitalism and upon social privilege, to those who are called to resist the insinuating overtures of supernatural evil and the tremendous

pressure of Nature upon the soul of man? What is the effect
of social, intellectual, and political debunking upon those
who see debunkers and debunked alike as pilgrims on a brief
terrestrial journey, with the ageless ages of eternity
enveloping them around?

One of the minor, and perhaps less lawful, pleasures of the
Christian's intellectual vision, is to see learned men laboriously discovering, or rabid radicals furiously declaiming,
simple platitudinous truths which he learned in childhood at
his mother's knee. Of course power corrupts. Of course there
is evil deep-seated in the soul of man. Of course the
rich and greedy and covetous are not happy. Of course you
cannot disfigure your world and exploit all its resources
thoughtlessly without doing damage to the face of Creation
and to the soul of man. Of course machinery makes men
mechanical. Of course the universe is bigger and more
wonderful than we thought it. Of course Newtonian physics,
Evolution, Determinism, Freudian psychology were not the
last word after all.

And of course, of course, the world's social, political, and
cultural organization is so faulty that the best men often fail,
the worst often succeed; the noble find themselves down-
trodden, the mean and trivial flourish like the green bay-tree.
Why, as Christians, we have always taken it for granted that
the criminal in the dock may be a better man a thousand
times than the judge who condemns him; that the rich
magnate may be in every way unworthy to lick the boots of
those who scrub his floors, wash his dishes, and mine his
coal; that the learned and honoured professor may lack the
intellectual insight of his charwoman and the wisdom of her
infant son.

We have always known all this, and much more that sets the
world's judgements topsy-turvy, the world's evaluations
upside down. It is perhaps worth-while to point out the

scratched paint to the householder who is surveying his collapsing roof; but you must not expect him to get very excited about it. Nor must you urge him to start work on it with a blow-lamp there and then. We want to serve our culture, we want our civilization to work—not because it is the only good we can conceive, and not because we are finally and securely at home in it—but because it is a great drama that we have been staged in, and it is good that we should play our parts well. It is the Church's right to remind us that the theatre is only a theatre and—if we heed her—to nourish us in our own proper persons to the real life outside its walls.